street*style*

ted polhemus

eet style

from
sidewalk
to catwalk

thames and hudson

First published to coincide with the exhibition
Streetstyle held at the Victoria and Albert Museum,
London, 1994 – 1995.

British Library Cataloguing-in-Publication Data

A catalogue record for this book is available from the
British Library

ISBN 0–500–27794–X

Printed and bound in Singapore by C. S. Graphics

contents

hanging out   6

trickle down bubble up   8

tribal styles   13

- zooties   17
- zazous   20
- caribbean style   21
- western style   23
- bikers   26
- hip cats & hipsters   28
- beats, beatniks & existentialists   30
- teddy boys   33
- modernists   38
- folkies   40
- rockabillies   41
- la dolce vita   44
- coffee-bar cowboys & ton-up boys   46
- surfers   48
- mods   50
- rockers   54
- rude boys & two-tone   58
- swinging london & the psychedelics   61
- hippies   64
- greasers   67
- skinheads   69
- funk   72

- glam   74
- rastafarians   76
- headbangers   80
- northern soul   84
- skaters   86
- punks   89
- new romantics   94
- goths   97
- casuals   100
- psychobillies   102
- pervs   103
- b-boys & flygirls   106
- raggamuffins & bhangra style   109
- new age travellers   112
- ravers   115
- acid jazz   118
- indie kids, cuties, grunge & riot grrrls   122
- technos & cyberpunks   124

the gathering of the tribes   128

the supermarket of style   130

flow chart   136

notes   138

further information   138

photographic credits   142

acknowledgments   143

index   143

hanging out

West Indian men on a streetcorner in Liverpool in 1949.

A street corner in Harlem, 1940.
Outside a South London café, 1952.
Greenwich Village, New York, 1958.
Outside the Ace Café, North Circular Road,
    London, 1962.
Downtown, Kingston, Jamaica, 1963.
Carnaby Street, London, 1965.
The beach at La Jolla, California, 1966.
The intersection of Haight and Ashbury,
    San Francisco, 1967.
World's End, the King's Road, London, 1976.
A street party in the South Bronx, 1977.
Brixton, South London, 1994.

Auspicious moments. The art of being at the right place at the right time. Just hanging around. Looking sharp. All dressed up and nowhere to go. Doing nothing in particular. Making history.

Without the Hipsters, Teddy Boys, Beats, Rockers, Rude Boys, Mods, Surfers, Hippies, Punks, B-Boys, Flygirls, Raggamuffins – and all the other streetstyle originals – most of us would be left without anything to wear.

But the sharp suits, leather jackets, jeans, kaftans, flares, DMs, click suits and so forth are only the visible, tangible part of this legacy. Oozing through the clothes, hairstyles, make-up and accessories is an *attitude*. An attitude which perhaps more than any other sets the tone of life in the late twentieth century. In spirit if not in practice – like all those people in ads for Coke, Pepsi, Levi's and a thousand other products – we are out there, checking out the action, hanging around.

The Street is both the stage upon which this drama unfolds and the bottom line metaphor for all that is presumed to be real and happening in our world today. In the past, 'Western culture' was most at ease and most recognizable within grand interiors. Today, as high culture has given way to popular culture, it is the litmus test of 'street credibility' that is crucial. If it won't cut it on the corner, forget it.

Made back in 1933, the film *42nd Street* was an enticing preview of the role of The Street as a focus of modern life. Busby Berkeley's breathtaking finale begins with Ruby Keeler tap-dancing on the roof of a taxi. Panning down and sideways, the camera then takes us on a tour of a magical re-creation of 42nd Street. All human life is here. Mingling. Checking each other out. Doing their thing. There is mayhem, madness – even murder – but the excitement and the sense of 'This is where it's at' is so tangible that you want to reach out and grab handfuls of it. Instead of just passing through 42nd Street en route to somewhere else, we want to linger here. It is a destination as well as a thoroughfare.

Although The Street is a place, it isn't just any place. Busby Berkeley's film wouldn't have worked as *Fifth Avenue*. Nor as one of those elegant boulevards along which fashionable Parisians loved to promenade at the turn of the century. Though the promenade might have marked a critical moment in the shift from inside to outside, it shouldn't by any means be confused with hanging out.

To promenade is to hob-nob with those on the up and up. Hanging out, on the other hand, is best done in the company of those from the wrong side of the tracks. Some *low life* is essential. That, and youth: *juvenile* delinquents. In this sense, The Street is a dead end – the place to go when you aren't old enough or rich enough to get in somewhere.

But while practical necessity may make The Street a last resort for some, it is precisely this quality which makes it so seductive for many who could be elsewhere. The allure of The Street as a road to nowhere is perfectly captured in Francis Ford Coppola's 1983 cult film *Rumble Fish*. Rusty James, the Motorcycle Boy, Smoke and their friends are the personification of low life: tragically flawed, angst-ridden, dead-end kids. No-hopers. But when they hit The Street, we – like Steve, the only guy with a future – just have to join them.

Like the colourblind Motorcycle Boy, we see The Street in dazzling black and white: the flickering neon signs, the kids playing in the gush of water from the fire hydrant, the hookers, the pimps, the bottle-toting drunks. Up what is literally a dead-end alley we are attacked by thugs and left for dead. But we'll be back because we just can't resist the seductiveness of The Real Thing.

'Nowhere to go accounts for groups of Teddy Boys hanging about the streets in South London' – the original caption to this 1955 photograph.

Postmodern theorists from Frederic Jameson to Jean Baudrillard see the elusiveness of authenticity as the fundamental crisis of our age. And who can doubt them? 'The Real Thing' sold a lot of Coke and it is this same insatiable craving for authenticity that lures us onto The Street with Rusty James and the Motorcycle Boy. There is a fundamental irony in this which shouldn't escape us. These no-hopers have none of those things that our society officially decrees to be important (money, prestige, success, fame) and yet they have a monopoly on what we're actually most in need of – The Real.

This is the key to The Street's seductive appeal. And, of course, to the appeal of streetstyle. Like holy relics, streetstyle garments radiate the power of their associations. Every age uses dress and body decoration to signal what is most important at that historical moment. Throughout most of our history that message has been, 'I am rich,' or, 'I am powerful.' If today more and more people use their dress style to assert: 'I am authentic,' it is simply evidence of our hunger for the genuine article in an age which seems to so many to be one of simulation and hype.

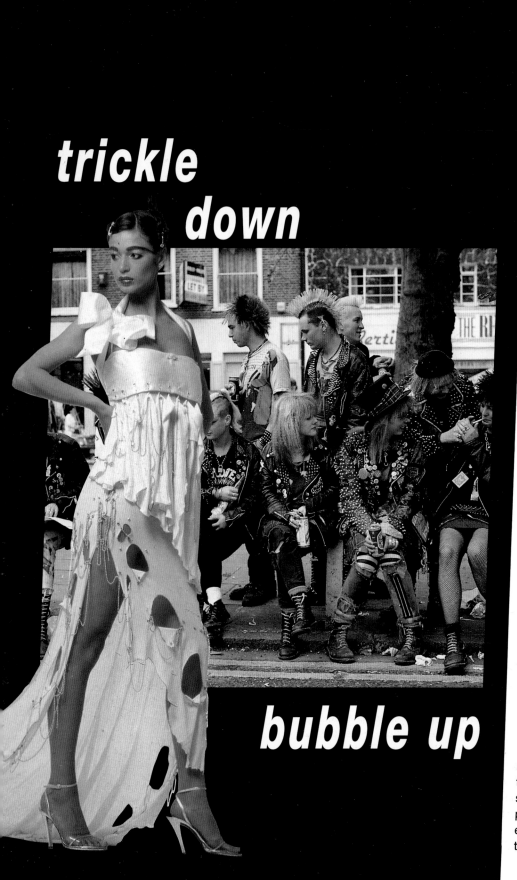

trickle down

bubble up

Styles which start life on the streetcorner have a way of ending up on the backs of top models on the world's most prestigious fashion catwalks. This shouldn't surprise us because, as we have seen, the authenticity which streetstyle is deemed to represent is a precious commodity. Everyone wants a piece of it.

But it is more than the price tag which distinguishes the genuine article from its chic reinterpretation. It's a question of context. And when fashion sticks its metaphorical gilt frame around a leather motorbike jacket, a Hippy kaftan, a pair of trainers, or a Ragga girl's batty-riders, it transforms an emblem of subcultural identity into something which anyone with enough money can acquire and wear with pride.

However much streetstyle and fashion might superficially resemble each other, they are actually poles apart. Fashion is trendy. It celebrates change and progress. Change, because This Year's New Look always elbows aside Last Year's New Look in a perpetual pursuit of novelty. Progress, because of the implicit assumption – one which characterizes modern society – that The New is also – by definition, *ipso facto* – The Improved. Both a product of modernism and its ultimate expression, fashion faces resolutely towards the future. It has the capacity to generate the new and fresh, a capacity which has always made it appealing to those who subscribe to the view that change is preferable to the status quo and that tomorrow holds more promise than yesterday. (And when in the eighties there was a widespread swing towards a *post*-modernism which cast doubt on such progressive assumptions, this was reflected in a corresponding shift away from ever-changing fashion and towards classic, anti-trendy style.)

In its heyday (for example, in the 1950s and 1960s), fashion managed to get practically everyone to fall in line behind the particular look which it decreed to be *the* trend. As Peter York puts it in *Modern Times*:

Fashion had its own establishment, a kind of Vatican, in the fifties and sixties and in this set-up they had dictators who set the lines for everybody to follow.

The lines were set like edicts in the way of the old world . . . They were set by magazine editors for magazine readers. Vogue used to announce the colour of the season and up and down the land shops presented clothes in banana beige or coral red or whatever.

In the fifties there were actually lines for fashion. Dictates about the shape a woman's clothes should be, irrespective of the shape of her. And then came the sixties. Remember the mini . . .

And the point was that everyone wore it, your sister, your auntie, the gym mistress, everyone.

For truly THERE WAS NO ALTERNATIVE.[1]

We find an even more illuminating example of the fashion system in action if we turn the clock back just a little further, to 1947, when Christian Dior launched his 'New Look' on a world still waiting for the dust to settle on the Second World War. If ever there was a time when people yearned to catch a glimpse of a promising future, this was it, and the 'New Look', though actually a re-working of an old look, certainly seemed fresh and novel compared to the dress women had been obliged to wear throughout the war.

Using extravagant amounts of fabric in its long, full skirts and cinching in women's waists in a way which some saw as unliberated, Dior's design raised many an eyebrow and prompted many a politician to rail against its profligacy. But such opposition was, of course, doomed to failure. For here was the spirit of The New at a time when everyone was desperate to be rid of The Old.

Of course only a tiny minority of women were in a position to purchase one of Dior's creations, but the years following 1947 saw the New Look *'trickle down'* (indeed, in this case, cascade down) to the department stores and, very quickly, to patterns which could be run up at home. However difficult it was to accomplish, women from Paris to Los Angeles and all points in between struggled to fall in step with the march of fashion. For, as Peter York correctly says, in those days THERE WAS NO ALTERNATIVE.

This classic example illustrates the three principal characteristics of fashion: its celebration of The New, its singularity (*the* New Look) and its diffusion from high society to mass market. But today, while stories of the death of fashion (my own included) may have been exaggerated, all three of these characteristics seem much less in evidence than they were only a few decades ago.

Firstly, as one might expect in a 'Postmodern Age', a growing number of people seem dubious about the proposition that what is new is necessarily improved. Such distrust in progress is hardly surprising at a time when environmental, economic and social realities cast such a dark shadow on the future. This shift in attitude has influenced developments in interior and furniture design, as well as in architecture – most notably in a renewed emphasis on 'Reconstruction'. Likewise, in the sphere of clothing and accessory design, 'timeless classics' have gained in popularity. Indeed, those who jump uncritically on the latest bandwagon have been branded 'fashion victims', while the word 'trendy' has often become a put-down rather than a compliment.

Secondly, instead of the authority of *the* fashion, one is today more likely to see pluralism, with different designers proposing radically conflicting New Looks. While some fashion pundits may strive to reduce this cacophony of different colours, shapes, hemlengths and so on, into a consistent trend – a single 'direction' – anyone viewing the photographs of the Paris, Milan, London or New York shows can appreciate that difference, rather than consensus, is the order of the day.

Such multiplicity of 'direction', coupled with an apparently growing inclination on the

Riding the waves of the 1990s 'Punk Revival' – Gianni Versace's 1994 evening dress held together with jewelled safety pins. Photo: Niall McInerney.

Above: Classic 'Perfecto'/'Bronx' style black leather motorcycle jacket, available from a Lewis Leathers catalogue, early 1960s.

Right: Long live rock 'n' roll! Homage to Gene Vincent in DIY leather jacket art, King's Road, London, 1981.

part of many simply to wear what suits them rather than to swallow fashion's prescription, has brought a variety of dress and adornment styles which is arguably without equal in history. The homogeneity of appearance which Peter York (in the quote above) sees as characteristic of, for example, the sixties ('everyone wore it, your sister, your auntie, the gym mistress, everyone') is no longer typical. Today, when you look at what people are actually wearing on the street, in the office and at nightclubs, what is obvious is that now there *is* an alternative. Indeed, lots and lots of alternatives, as the 'edicts' of yesteryear are pushed aside by the demands of personal choice.

Finally, do new looks still begin life within high fashion and 'trickle down' for mass consumption? It is undoubtedly true that the mass-market 'mainline' fashion industry continues to take a lead from the more exclusive, highly priced designers. But do the creations we see on those exclusive, cameraflashlit catwalks all originate in the minds of the world's top designers?

Not on the evidence that I see. To my eyes an increasingly frequent chain of events goes like this. First there is a genuine streetstyle innovation. This may be featured in a pop music video and streetkids in other cities and countries may pick up on the style. Then, finally – at the end rather than the beginning of the chain – a ritzy version of the original idea makes an appearance as part of a top designer's collection.

Instead of trickle-down, *bubble up*. Instead of the bottom end of the market emulating the top end, precisely the reverse.

If Dior's 'New Look' illustrates the traditional trickle-down process, then the 'Perfecto' motorcycle jacket (also known as the 'Bronx' jacket) may serve to illustrate the bubble-up process in action. Based on a World War II design, the Perfecto jacket as made by the Schott Brothers company of New York became the symbol of rebellious youth when Marlon Brando wore one in *The Wild One*. With its sinister black sheen and its zips like knife slashes, this garment embodied an attitude and lifestyle which directly challenged 'normal society'.

In the suburban American community in which I grew up in the fifties and sixties, the only kids who wore such jackets hung out at the pool hall 'looking for trouble'. This was *Rumble Fish* territory – deep on the wrong side of town.

While I can recall secretly admiring these jackets early in the sixties, it would be well into the seventies before I actually got up the nerve to buy one. Nor was such hesitancy based entirely on unjustified paranoia. As shown in *American Graffiti*'s portrayal of teenage life in the USA of the early sixties – where the hero's madras sports jacket contrasts tellingly with his tormentors' Perfecto style jackets – this garment marked a very real subcultural (and often socio-economic) boundary.

In Britain, a similar jacket was made by Lewis Leathers. Mick Farren, a braver soul than myself, got it together to buy himself one when he was only fifteen:

I bought the jacket in a small, backstreet men's clothing store, hard up against a railway bridge in a medium sized seaside

An extraordinary number of fashion designers have translated the basic design of the 'Perfecto'/'Bronx' black leather jacket from the street to the catwalk. Shown here *from left to right* are examples from Katharine Hamnett's Winter 1990 collection, John Richmond's Spring/Summer 1993 collection and Gianni Versace's Spring/Summer 1994 collection. Photos Niall McInerney.

town in southern England. It was hardly the concrete jungle but it passed at the time. The store specialized in tacky, juvenile delinquent fashions – polkadot shirts, stardust peggies, dayglo socks and lurid suits that usually fell apart after a couple of weeks . . . I stood in front of the store's full-length mirror and slipped off whatever jacket I was wearing. (It isn't part of the memory. It was probably some flakey tweed sportcoat of which my mother totally approved.) I struggled into what was going to be my first cool garment . . . The jacket came from D. Lewis Ltd of Great Portland Street, London. It was the Bronx model. As I stared into the mirror, I couldn't believe myself. Admittedly the mirror was tilted up to produce the most flattering effect, but I looked great. My legs seems longer, my shoulders seemed broader. I flipped the collar up. I looked so damned

cool. Mother of God, I was a cross between Elvis and Lord Byron.[2]

Only very gradually, throughout the seventies and into the eighties, did the black leather motorbike jacket become accepted as everyday, 'normal' apparel. Arguably the most potent indicator of how streetstyle in general has gradually become an accepted part of our culture, its wider appeal was guaranteed when it became *de rigueur* for serious rock musicians. From Gene Vincent to Jim Morrison, from Lou Reed to The Clash, from Bruce Springsteen to George Michael, the black leather jacket is there to assure us of a musician's authenticity.

What makes the Perfecto The Real Thing is its Bad Boy/Girl, wrong-side-of-the-tracks image. That and the fact that it is a classic, anti-fashion garment, virtually unchanged in its design for some five decades.

But what is true of the genuine article as made by the Schott Brothers or Lewis Leathers is not true of the countless imitations which began appearing on high fashion catwalks in the 1980s. First it was the 'street cred' designers like Katharine Hamnett, Pam Hogg and Jean-Paul Gaultier who produced their own jazzed-up versions. But when, by the mid-eighties, high fashion designers like Claude Montana, Thierry Mugler, Gianni Versace and Sonia Rykiel showed versions of the Perfecto, the bubble-up process was well and truly complete.

The transformation of the Perfecto style jacket from subcultural emblem to high and mainstream fashion is hardly unique. Most of the dozens of streetstyles dealt with in this book have at some time, in some way, provided inspiration for a wide range of fashion designers. Indeed, we have come to

For his Autumn/Winter 1989/90 collection fashion designer Jean-Paul Gaultier changed the 'Perfecto' from black to dazzling gold but retained its distinctive style features in order to signal 'street credibility'.
Photo: Niall McInerney.

expect that styles which begin life on dead-end, mean streets will almost instantaneously and with ever-increasing regularity make an appearance on even the most prestigious of fashion catwalks. And, in the process, the pages of *Vogue* and *Elle* have often come to resemble those of *The Face* and *i-D* (but with the difference that the former's 'Punks', 'Raggamuffins', 'Travellers' and so forth are actually highly paid models styled in some fantasized imitation of The Real Thing).

On one level this inversion of the socio-economic order is all very admirable. Who wants to return to a time when the social élite were so full of themselves that they refused to believe that anything of value could come from those further down the ladder? It was the sixties which at long last recognized that culture is not the prerogative of the upper classes – a realization which revitalized our society with creative talent and new blood.

The bubble-up process has made us a fully fledged creative democracy in which talent isn't thought to be limited by class or race or education or how much money you've got in the bank. For our culture as a whole it is surely all for the best that the full spectrum of creative energy in our society has been tapped.

However, those who are actually members of such stylistically influential subcultures may not share this enthusiasm for the bubble-up process. Both in 1977, when Zandra Rhodes presented her ripped and safety-pinned 'Punk Look', and, more recently, when Versace and other high fashion designers produced similarly derivative styles, genuine Punks of my acquaintance usually categorized such imitation as 'insult' rather than flattery. Likewise, Johnny Stuart, author of the definitive book on Rockers, recently commented that

It is irritating to see how the leather jacket has become just a fashion garment. I can remember how back in the days when Rockers were far, far outnumbered by Mods, to wear your leathers was a risky business indeed. If you weren't careful, if you didn't stay on your bike and keep moving, your leather jacket could get ripped off your back

and you could get a real beating. The fancy fashionable versions of the Perfecto which you see all over the place these days water down the significance of the thing, taking away its original magic, castrating it.[3]

Even within the fashion industry there is concern at what is seen as 'exploitation' of streetstyle creativity. According to British designer Joe Casely-Hayford,

The fashion world has become so hungry that people are scouring – they come from all over the world to London, taking aspects of different groups and using it, consuming it and moving on to the next thing. But the fashion world will continue to miss the essence and will continue to exploit and will continue to rape and will continue to move on in a very superficial and trivial way.[4]

Strong words. But then the implication and effects of the bubble-up process cannot be taken lightly. Imitation may be the sincerest form of flattery, but just as the counterfeiting of fashion designers' own designs undermines their value, something similar occurs when fashion copies streetstyle. That authenticity and sense of subcultural identity which is symbolized in streetstyle is lost when it becomes 'this year's latest fashion' – something which can be purchased and worn without reference to its original subcultural meaning. In this sense, what may begin as a designer's genuinely felt desire to celebrate 'the street' as a wellspring of fresh ideas may have the inadvertent effect of undermining the 'street value' of these styles for the very people who originally created them.

The annual British Tattoo Festival in Dunstable, England. A semicircle of men in motorbike boots, jeans, T-shirts and battered, cut-off leather jackets has formed around one of the many tattooists' booths. In the centre a similarly dressed young man is acting as nonchalant as possible while the electric needle buzzes loudly over his upper arm. Why all this interest in what appears to be quite a small tattoo?

It turns out that this is a rite of passage. The guy in the chair is becoming a member of the Bracknell Chopper Club. The tattoo, an elegant pair of gold wings, is the club's insignia. Everyone watching except myself has an identical design on his left bicep. Noticing that the same insignia appears on their leather jackets, I ask the guy next to me why duplication in the form of a tattoo is necessary:

'A tattoo's for life. And so is joining the club. We're all in this for good. Understand?'

The members of the Bracknell Chopper Club and this significant event vividly demonstrate the difference between fashion and style. These men are not fashion victims. We can see this in their clothing – the most treasured items being those which are the oldest (and which look it). And any permanent body decoration like a tattoo is as anti-fashion as it is possible to get – literally making change difficult if not impossible. When one and then two years later I notice these same men at subsequent tattoo conventions they look exactly the same except for a few additional tattoos and some grey hairs.

Style isn't trendy. Quite the opposite. It's inherently conservative and traditional and it is for this reason that it often makes use of permanent body decorations. The intricate tattoos of the Maori and other peoples of the South Pacific, the scarification patterns of various African peoples, the enormous lip plugs found in parts of the Amazon and the tattooed insignia of the Bracknell Chopper Club all serve to resist change.

And to mark membership in a social group. In all probability styles of body decoration have served to distinguish 'Us'

tribal styles

***Top*: Members of the Bracknell Chopper Club, photographed by the author at the annual Tattoo Festival in Dunstable, Bedfordshire, in 1987.**

***Above*: A detail showing the distinctive tattoo which marks membership of this club.**

from 'Them' throughout history and we can see this important function of style at work in any of those tribal societies which survive today. Different colours of body paint, different designs, different adornments provide an immediately recognizable visual guide as to who is a member of which tribal group.

The history of streetstyle is a history of 'tribes'. Zooties, Hipsters, Beats, Rockers, Hippies, Rude Boys, Punks . . . right up to today's Travellers and Raggamuffins are all *subcultures* which use a distinctive style of dress and decoration to draw a line between 'Us' and 'Them'.

What's intriguing about this is the fact that such *styletribes* have blossomed and flourished at precisely that time in history when individuality and personal freedom have come to be seen as the defining features of our age. As Margaret Thatcher told us, 'Today there is no such thing as society. There are just individuals and their families.' And by and large this is something she was right about. The old groupings of class, region, religion and ethnic background have decreased in importance, leaving the individual free to pursue life as he or she personally chooses.

Why should anyone want to give up this freedom to join a group like the Bracknell Chopper Club? Or, on a larger scale, groups like Rockers, Mods, Hippies, Punks, Goths and Raggamuffins?

My view is that the tribal imperative is and always will be a fundamental part of human nature. Like our most distant ancestors we feel alienated and purposeless when we do not experience this sense of belonging and comradeship. It is no coincidence that the decline of traditional social groupings which has intensified so markedly since the Second World War precisely parallels the rise of a new type of social group, the *styletribe*. Hipsters, Teddy Boys, Mods, Rockers and so forth arose to satisfy that need for a sense of community and common purpose which is so lacking in modern life.

So it comes as no surprise that these styletribes are particularly attractive to teenagers. It is during the adolescent years that a person is moving apart from his or her parental family while not yet having formed a new family. If contemporary life was made up of more than 'individuals and their families', this would not be a problem. But in our anti-society society the teenager steps out of the parental family into a social vacuum.

The simplest way to fill this vacuum is the *gang* – a small group with a territory (a 'home turf') and, typically, a distinctive style of dress ('colours') to set it apart from other gangs and from the mainstream. This situation is vividly portrayed in the film *The Warriors* (1979), which opens with an attempted reconciliation between some ten different New York street gangs. The Warriors themselves wear black leather waistcoats with their vivid insignia painted on the back. Another gang wears Hawaiian shirts and Panama hats. Another, baseball uniforms and blue facepaint. And still another dresses in a style reminiscent of *Clockwork Orange,* with white facepaint, top hats and braces.

Styletribes are also marked out by a distinctive appearance style but their enormous scale and national or even international boundaries indicate a uniquely

Skinheads in High Wycombe, Buckinghamshire, 1985. Photo: Gavin Watson.

modern approach to 'tribal' identity. While all the members of a gang (or, for that matter, a 'real' tribe) know and are personally involved with each other, the vast majority of the members of styletribes are complete strangers – linked together only by reports in the media, by pop music role models and by a shared style of dress and adornment.

How do styletribes form and how do they function? Let us look at one example – the Punks. In London, in 1975 and into 1976, a small clique of young people (many known as the Bromley Set because they came from Bromley, in Kent) began to meet up in various places at the less prestigious end of the King's Road. Vivienne Westwood and Malcolm McLaren's shop SEX was one such meeting place and the unusual items of clothing on sale there (for example, fetish garments in rubber and PVC) provided a stylistic focus. The number of kids involved was small – at a guess, no more than a couple of hundred. Most were known to each other and in this sense, at this point in time, they were a gang rather than a styletribe.

When the media began to take an interest in these early proto-Punks (and especially when McLaren's rock group, the Sex Pistols, outraged the public via a notorious TV appearance), a stereotype began to form of a typical 'Punk Rocker'. Thanks to this publicity, young people throughout Britain began to imitate this style. Within a few months there were thousands of Punks spread across the UK – and, before long, hundreds of thousands of Punks as far afield as Berlin, Barcelona, Rome, New York, LA and Tokyo. These have more recently spread into Eastern Europe.

Sharing (at least at first glance) only an appearance style and an interest in a new form of rock music, thousands of Punks scattered between different cities, countries and continents would hardly seem to qualify as a subculture, let alone a 'tribe'. But this view forgets that style is a wonderfully expressive medium – capable of representing complex ideas, attitudes and values.

It is impossible fully to translate the meaning of the appearance style of Punks or any other styletribe into words. Nevertheless,

London Punks on the King's Road in 1980, submitting to the camera for the umpteenth time.

when we compare, for example, the Punks' style with that of the Hippies, we immediately appreciate the extent to which these express very different worldviews. The Punks' black leather, fetishistic garments, studs and Crazy Colour hairstyles indicate a nihilism, an aggressive stance and a delight in artifice and deliberate perversity which is a complete opposite to the Hippies' new-age, love-&-peace, back-to-nature philosophy (itself perfectly expressed in the form of typical Hippy dress and adornment).

Style isn't just a superficial phenomenon. It's the visible tip of something much greater. And encoded within its iconography are all those ideas and ideals which together constitute a (sub)culture. Like-looking is like-thinking and in this sense the members of a styletribe have a great deal in common.

Nor should we forget that the decision to dress and adorn oneself in an extreme or unusual manner is no trivial matter. The Punks who dyed their hair green or even the Hippies who let their hair grow long at a time when short hair was the norm were risking a great deal – job prospects, family harmony, verbal and sometimes even physical abuse. To adopt the look of a particular styletribe is

to put oneself on the firing line. But if such stylistic commitment brings a sense of group solidarity and comradeship, then, for many, it is worth it.

Like all tribes, styletribes hope that they will be timeless, unchanging. It is this wish which leads the members of many styletribes to make use of the permanent body arts like tattooing. While mainstream society attempts to dismiss such subcultures as 'just a fad', those within them want to believe that their tribe will carry on 'forever'. History, however, has frequently revealed the futility of this dream. 'Punk's Not Dead' may have been the rallying cry heard a decade after Punk first began but by that time one was more likely (at least in Britain) to encounter Punks on postcards than in real life.

It is easy to conclude, therefore, that Punk was just a passing fashion in a history of youthculture which is more often than not typified by transience. Such a view, however, does not entirely fit the facts. Firstly, the *spirit* of Punk is very much alive, to the extent that its style and attitude have influenced other contemporary styletribes and even mainstream culture (more about which in subsequent chapters). Secondly, in countries

Right: **A group of original Teddy Boys in 1955? No, members of The Edwardian Drape Society (T.E.D.S.) in Clapham Junction, London, 1993. Photo: Sarah Tierney.**

Below right: **Japanese Kajis – 'Casuals' who draw stylistic inspiration from American workwear – in Shibuya, Tokyo, 1992. Photo: Norbert Schoerner.**

other than the UK – from Germany to Japan, the USA to Russia – small but flourishing Punk communities continue to exist. Finally, even in Britain, where media overkill and the stigma of classification as a tourist attraction had a negative effect in the 1980s, a new generation which was not even born when 'Anarchy in the UK' first appeared is producing a tiny but enthusiastic new Punk subculture.

A similar story could be told regarding Teddy Boys, Mods, Rockers, Skinheads, Rockabillies, Hipsters, Surfers, Hippies, Rastafarians, Headbangers, Goths and many others. In traditional historical terms, it is still early days, but already it is clear that both individually and as a generic social phenomenon styletribes cannot be dismissed as something transitory. In practice as well as in hope, such groups and the appearance styles which they create to express their shared values and beliefs remain as an exception to the rule of our culture's mercurial inclinations.

**A Zootie in Harlem setting, circa 1942.
Illustration: Chris Sullivan.**

There are two basic moves in streetstyle: Dressing Up and Dressing Down. The predominantly middle-class Beatniks and Hippies illustrate the latter tendency – using dress to make a symbolic descent of the socio-economic ladder in the interests of authenticity. The Zooties illustrate the former. The zoot suit, with its extravagant use of expensive fabric and its luxurious accessories, loudly proclaimed the message: 'I've got it made'. This message has an obvious attraction to the underprivileged, and one such underprivileged black man was Malcolm X. In his autobiography he describes his initiation in the early 1940s into the world of the zoot-suited hipsters :

I was measured, and the young salesman picked off a rack a zoot suit that was just wild: sky-blue pants thirty inches in the knee and angle-narrowed down to twelve inches at the bottom, and a long coat that pinched my waist and flared out below my knees. As a gift, the salesman said, the store would give me a narrow leather belt with my initial 'L' on it. Then he said I ought to also buy a hat, and I did – blue, with a feather in the four-inch brim. Then the store gave me another present: a long, thick-lined, gold-plated chain that swung down lower than my coat hem . . . I took three of those twenty-five-cent sepia-toned, while-you-wait pictures of myself, posed the way 'hipsters' wearing their zoots would 'cool it' – hat angled, knees drawn close together, feet wide apart, both index fingers jabbed toward the floor."[1]

While the 'conked' (chemically straightened) hair which Malcolm X and other African-Americans of the 1940s adopted represented an acquiescence to white standards of appearance, the zoot suit

zooties

Right: Musician, artist, poet, club entrepreneur and man about town Chris Sullivan in a classic Zoot suit and accessories – a style which will always be associated with his band, Blue Rondo a La Turk.

Right: Musician, artist, poet, club entrepreneur and man about town Chris Sullivan in a classic Zoot suit and accessories – a style which will always be associated with his band, Blue Rondo a La Turk.

marked a significant moment in the development of a distinctive black American identity.

It is interesting (and not, perhaps, a matter of chance) that the focus of this emerging black cultural identity should be the male suit. In *The Psychology of Clothes*,[2] J. C. Flügel traced what he termed 'The Great Masculine Renunciation' of exotic adornment and apparel to the late eighteenth century, when most Western men (reacting, in Flügel's view, to the French Revolution) began to limit their appearance style to one which emphasized businesslike sobriety and respectability at the expense of experimentation and frivolity. Central to this transition was the male suit, which generally became an emblem of conformity, compliance with the work ethic, and

conservatism, and which symbolized the renunciation of that delight in bodily adornment which had in the past typified male appearance in the West.

In reinventing the suit as a showy, extrovert garment, the Zooties were breaking free of 'The Great Masculine Renunciation' and also, in the process, establishing their appearance style as 'an emblem of ethnicity and a way of negotiating an identity. The zoot suit was a refusal: a subcultural gesture that refused to concede to the manners of subservience.'[3]

This was true not only of African-Americans but also of the young Mexican-Americans who had poured into Southern California in the 1930s and 1940s. Finding little to identify with in either their parents' Hispanic culture or the Great American

The definitive Zootie, Cab Calloway, in the 1943 all-singing, all-dancing film *Stormy Weather*.

Dream, these 'Pachucos' wore their zoot suits as an emblem of a new subcultural pride and rebellion.

But though the Pachucos were numerous and distinctive, the impact of their style was limited because, to most of America, Mexican-Americans remained an invisible minority. Precisely the opposite was true of the black Zooties for the simple reason that their subcultural uniform was adopted as the standard attire of many of the popular jazz musicians of the time.

So great was the influence from jazz that in 1941 the *New Yorker* magazine predicted that the zoot suit would define the direction of mainstream male fashion:

We herewith submit a preview of men's Easter fashions from the world's least inhibited fashion centre, Harlem. Trousers will be deeply pleated with waistband just under the armpits, 30-inch knees, and 15-inch cuffs. A popular suit jacket is one that measures 36 inches down the back seam and has a fly front, shoulders padded out 3½ inches on each side, two breast pockets, and slashed

Zootie revivalist Kid Creole performing at the Lyceum, London, 1982. Photo: David Corio.

side pockets. This may be worn with a white doeskin waistcoat. Shoes are pointed, the most popular leathers being light-tan calfskin and coloured suede. Hats may be worn in the porkpie shape or with crowns 6 inches high. Colours, as always, are limited only by spectrum.'[4]

Did this white, middle-class magazine seriously think that its male readers would adopt such an uninhibited style or was it just making a joke at the expense of black men? I would guess the latter. But it was precisely at this historic moment that the threat of war rendered the issue academic: in March 1942 the War Production Board ruled that the wool used in men's suits must be reduced by 26 percent, thereby defining the zoot suit as unpatriotic, even illegal.

And thereby, at a stroke, denying young African- and Mexican-Americans their newfound badge of subcultural identity. In fact, however, they ignored the WPB's ruling and found plenty of compliant backstreet tailors who, if the price was right, were willing to turn a blind eye to cloth rationing. For over

a year Zooties continued to thumb their noses at the war effort, but they were to pay a high price for their bravado. In 1943 some of Southern California's white servicemen decided that it was their patriotic duty to beat up Hispanic and black youths who openly flouted the WPB restrictions. According to Stuart Cosgrove:

It became commonplace for gangs of marines to ambush zoot-suiters, strip them down to their underwear and leave them helpless in the streets. In one particularly vicious incident, a gang of drunken sailors rampaged through a cinema after discovering two zoot-suiters. They dragged the pachucos on to the stage as the film was being screened, stripped them in front of the audience and, as a final insult, urinated on the suits.[5]

In June 1943 Los Angeles witnessed its first fully-fledged riots as Pachucos of both sexes (for by this time there were also all-female gangs like 'The Slick Chicks' and 'The Black Widows', who wore zoot-suit jackets, black skirts and fishnets) fought white servicemen and policemen. The riots spread east to cities in Arizona, Texas . . . then to Detroit, Philadelphia and New York.

So what had begun as aspirational Dressing Up and as a marker of youthful subcultures suddenly became a focus of racial identity. Although Malcolm X would later describe the Zootie as a 'clown',[6] the fact remains that the 'zoot suit riots' served to sow the seeds of that sense of black and Hispanic consciousness which would blossom to profound effect in the 1960s.

In addition to this, the Zooties set in motion a sense of stylistic/subcultural identity which was to permeate the entire history of streetstyle. To wear a zoot in 1943 was to put yourself on the line and within this context the garment became a uniform in the full sense of the word – a badge of defiance, a marker of community and an ideological statement. Above all else, it is this idea of appearance as

something more than 'looking nice' which defines streetstyle.

Meanwhile, 1943 also saw the release of the all-singing, all-dancing, all-black film Stormy Weather. No riots here. Everything is hunky-dory as the ever-smiling Bill Robinson hosts a gala event 'for the soldiers'. The curtain parts and Cab Calloway makes his entrance. He is, in a sense, that 'clown' whom Malcolm X saw as undermining African-American dignity. But in his immaculate zoot suit, feathered fedora and spotless white shoes he is also undeniably magnificent. As such, he and his fellow Zooties constituted a direct, much needed challenge to that white, Western prescription that dignity and a resplendent, stylish appearance are incompatible elements of masculinity.

The entire history of streetstyle demonstrates the significance of this legacy, with male Bikers, Rockabillies, Teddy Boys, Hippies, Mods, Rude Boys, Glam Rockers, Punks, B-Boys, Goths, Raggamuffins and so on, all – in their own way – demonstrating the grace and pride of the male peacock. For this we should all be grateful. No jive.

The ORIGINAL **zoot suit** now available from SULLIVAN'S SUITS (PARADISE GARAGE) 3a Haymarket Walk Bristol 1 tel. 0272 290280

This mail-order advertisement, which appeared in the New Musical Express in 1982, reflects the enthusiasm of many of the New Romantics for Zootie style.

Swing! A dancing Zazou in Paris in the early 1940s shows how the French interpreted American Zootie style.

zazous

Surprisingly – given the racial cross-over and the geographic distance – the most extreme emulation of Zootie style took place in Paris. There, in the early 1940s, a fascination with Cab Calloway and other exponents of 'swing' led to the formation of a small but influential subculture which became known as the Zazous.

Probably never numbering more than a few hundred, the Zazous were divided into two separate factions: Left Bank and Right Bank. On the Left Bank, styles were scruffier and attitudes more bohemian – an alternative appearance was used as a badge of rebellion in a manner which paved the way for the Existentialists. On the Champs-Elysées, however, an immaculate elegance prevailed, combined with no more than a pretence of intellectual inclination. Here, male Zazous wore huge zoot jackets with many vents and pockets, bright handkerchiefs, high collars and very narrow ties held tightly in place by a gold pin. Trousers were worn above the ankle to show off white or brightly coloured socks and platform-soled shoes. A tightly rolled umbrella was essential. Most striking of all, their hair, styled with the help of lashings of cooking oil, culminated in a gravity defying quiff or tuft at the front.

Female Zazous sported a similarly precarious style – typically featuring a large, square bun positioned above the forehead. They also wore roomy zoot jackets with padded shoulders. Polo-neck sweaters, narrow ties, short pleated skirts and platform shoes which were as wide as they were high completed the outfit.

The immediate inspiration for their distinctive name appears to have been the refrain of French crooner Johnny Hess's hit 'I'm Swing' which went something like 'Za zou, za zou, za zou, za zou ze'. A more seminal candidate, however, might be Cab Calloway's earlier hit, 'Zaz Zuh Zaz'.

The various reports of the Zazous suggest a style-obsessed, fun-loving group of young people, not unlike the New Romantics of the 1980s. What sets the Zazous apart, however, is the fact that they did their narcissistic thing right in the middle of the German occupation of Paris. Not surprisingly, the Germans weren't very taken with these 'decadent' young people who looked to the USA for inspiration and the Zazous were continually mocked by the collaborationist press.

The immediate issue, of course, was their open defiance of clothing rationing, which the German occupiers had established in 1941 to limit both the number of new garments purchased and the amount of fabric used in their manufacture. But, in a more generalized sense, it seems that what most rattled the Germans was the Zazous' general unwillingness to act as if there was a war on.

In July 1942 a collaborationist French youth group known as Jeunesse Populaire Française decided to 'Scalp the Zazous' and, armed with hairclippers, they set about their patriotic task – an eerie precursor of the attacks by white American servicemen less than a year later on the Pachucos and black Zooties of southern California.

Finally, as the collaborationist press stepped up its campaign to have the Zazous sent to work camps, most went into hiding and by 1945, when France was liberated, there were few Zazous to be seen. Although they never re-formed as a group, their name lived on in France after the war as a way of describing anyone whose style of dress was slightly out of the ordinary. More significantly, however, as Farid Chenoune suggests in *A History of Men's Fashion*, their existence constituted 'a little Copernican revolution in male fashion fomented by what was already being called "youth culture"'.[1] Or, as those unusually dressed 'petit swings' would have put it . . . 'Zazouzazouzazouze!'

caribbean style

Perez Pantalon Prado – 'King of the Cha-Cha-Cha' – demonstrates his dancing skills in Paris in 1955, partnered by Gisèle Robert. The cha-cha-cha, imported from Cuba, was a big hit in the French capital.

Before the Cuban Revolution, Havana served as a release valve for the pent-up desires of moralistic America. As well as cheap drink, prostitution and gambling, Havana offered music – not only indigenous forms, but also jazz, which brought a steady influx of (mostly black) musicians from the USA. Naturally they came dressed for the part – sporting the zoot suits and other flash styles which were all the rage back in Harlem, Chicago, New Orleans and Miami.

When Cubans themselves picked up on these styles they evolved in a distinctive way – in the detailing. But the basic premise of Dressing Up remained intact: this was clothing which shrieked rather than whispered, 'I've got it made'. As in Harlem, this flamboyance was accomplished by means of the extravagant use of fabric – typically in colours that were hard to maintain, like white and pastel shades.

And though mambo and other musical forms took jazz in new, specifically 'Latin' directions, the apparel of the musicians remained true to an aesthetic which had been defined in black America. (So much so that when in the 1950s these same musicians came to the USA they were typically closer to the original Zootie influenced style than were the new bebop Hipsters who, as we shall see, were emphasizing the eccentric over the purely ostentatious.)

Jazz was not, however, the only arbiter of Caribbean style in the 1940s. There had long been a steady migration of peoples back and forth between, for example, the West Indies

West Indian man looking for lodgings in London, 1949.

and America and this interchange (plus the all-pervasiveness of Hollywood cinema) brought new stylistic ideas. Catalogues like the one produced by Sears Roebuck were coveted on the most remote islands and American and British fashion magazines were thumbed over for inspiration.

This is not, however, to say that Caribbean style was simply a rehash of American or British style. Since the days of slavery, a large proportion of people throughout the Caribbean had been obliged to develop skills in dressmaking and tailoring which allowed them to create unique, personalized garments for themselves and their families. In addition, an extensive network of backstreet tailors in practically every neighbourhood offered an affordable alternative to buying standardized, off-the-peg clothes from retail outlets. Both these factors contributed to a tendency towards variety and individual creativity – producing unique originals rather than carbon copies.

This originality was much in evidence in the 1950s when large numbers of West Indians began to arrive in Britain. Although they were often insufficiently dressed for the climate (and often wearing bright colours which could not withstand the smog of London and Britain's other industrialized cities), these immigrants brought with them a rich diversity of dress styles which, over decades, would provide inspiration for British streetstyle (and, in my view, high fashion).

The question has often been asked: 'Why has Britain played such a major part in the history of streetstyle?' There are many different answers (rebellion against an intransigent class structure being an obvious one), but we can never overlook the fact that time and time again inspirational paths lead back to those black, West Indian traditions which favour diversity and creativity over 'off the peg' conformity. While in purely stylistic terms there are discordant leaps between the flamboyant dress of the first wave of West Indian immigrants, the more pared-down simplicity of the Rude Boys in the 1960s and the visual cacophony of the contemporary Raggamuffins, all are clearly rooted in the same tradition of personal innovation.

Born Leonard Slye, Roy Rogers became the most famous of the 1940s 'Singing Cowboys', who mythologized original Western Style into a look which even today constitutes a key component of streetstyle.

Clothes are dreams translated into fabric. This is as true of streetstyle as it is of the most expensive *haute couture*. The dreams may be personal (as in the zoot suit's proclamation of individual success) or they may be shared (as in the Hippies' vision of natural harmony in the Age of Aquarius). Western Style falls into the latter category. Indeed, it taps into the American Dream itself.

Streetstyle – essentially urban in character, typically requiring the streetcorner or the nightclub dance-floor as a stage – doesn't at first glance appear comfortably to embrace Western Style – a style whose natural habitat is the rolling plains and the prairie. But because streetstyle is an embodiment of dreams, its inspirations need never be limited to its actual environment. In the 1970s, after all, Funk and Glam styles reached out to distant galaxies. And in the 1930s and 1940s people in towns and cities across North America reached out to a mythic heritage of the great outdoors as a source of stylistic and ideological inspiration.

Why did Western Style appeal at this particular point in history? The reasons are many and varied. Firstly, the rapid urbanization of the thirties and forties left many new city dwellers homesick for a rural way of life which the Dust Bowl disaster, the Depression and the industrial needs of the war effort obliged them to leave behind. Secondly, Western Style reflected and celebrated a demographic shift away from the East Coast, which had previously monopolized American culture. Thirdly, the American South was striving to find itself a positive identity and various historical factors

conspired to make this most feasible if the imagery of the South*west* were emphasized at the expense of the Southeast. And, finally, at a time of great hardship, the cowboy's rugged determination and triumph over adversity offered a symbol which all Americans could cherish.

If the cowboy hadn't existed he would have had to have been invented. And, in a sense, he was. All those 'Singing Cowboy' epics and B-movies which Hollywood churned out between the mid-1930s and the mid-1940s were more concerned with mythmaking than with historical accuracy. This was especially true of the dress styles. Real cowboys had been paid low wages and had worked long, arduous hours doing dirty jobs. To imagine that they could have ended up looking like Gene Autry or Roy Rogers is absurd. But America needed a vision of itself and Hollywood happily obliged.

So too did the music industry. While 'country and western' had most of its musical roots in Appalachia and the American Southeast, its visual appearance quickly ditched 'hillbilly' styles for 'cowboy and western' accoutrements. As Patrick Carr puts it in 'The Changing Image of Country Music':

The country-cowboy connection . . . is absolutely artificial. There is no substantial reason on God's earth why American rural working people anywhere but in real cow country should think it perfectly natural to dude themselves up like the Cisco Kid come Saturday night.[1]

Carr cites the case of Hank Williams, who usually performed in a Western-Style suit, cowboy boots and a five-gallon stetson:

western style

But Hank doesn't sing a word about little *dogies or lonesome nights on the old prairie. In fact the element of fantasy, western or otherwise, is almost entirely lacking in his music.*[2]

Such is the power of myth. And as America plunged into the Second World War this particular myth played a crucial part in the symbolic and real unification of culturally distinct regions under the umbrella of 'One Nation Under God'. It kept Hollywood busy and it provided 'country' music with an identity which was acceptable outside the South and Southwest. The cowboy had 'won the West' in the nineteenth century; in the twentieth he would give America a common identity.

Stylistically, his legacy is without equal. What was worn by the 'singing cowboys' on stage and screen – the boots, the stetson, the embroidered shirt and jacket, the bootlace tie – rapidly became the streetstyle of a subculture which was originally principally confined to the American Southwest but which soon (generally sans the stetson) spread throughout the USA. And eventually to Britain – there is today, for example, a thriving subculture of cowboys and cowgirls who roam the ranges of Glasgow and London.

But the effect of Western Style is without equal because of the impact that it has had

outside its subcultural devotees. As early as 1947 the Sears Roebuck catalogue offered Western-Style 'Denim Dungarees' with 'red double stitching, copper rivets' and a matching 'Denim Jacket'. By the following year Sears offered a whole page of 'Blue Jeans Specially Cut For The Feminine Figure' and 'Yippee! Cowboy-style Blue Denim Saddle Pants' which 'Have that slick-fitting, Western look young Americans want!'[3]

From this date on, denim jeans would become the most ubiquitous streetstyle garment. They are now so commonplace that we must remind ourselves how revolutionary they once were. Not only did they mark a critical juncture in the seemingly unstoppable shift from formal to casual, they also constitute the first important example of Dressing Down, in which middle-class people adopt working-class style. (The mythologizing of the cowboy made him the first universally acceptable Working-Class Hero).

Interestingly, throughout the fifties, sixties and seventies, while this process of socio-economic Dressing Down was gaining ground within the middle classes, country and western musicians were steadily shifting to a style which was rather more Dressing Up. The most famous creator of this 'Rhinestone Cowboy' look was a New York Jewish ex-boxer-turned-tailor named 'Nudie' Cohen. Nudie had started out making clothes for

Top left: Classic Western style, as worn by Jim Reeves, 1954.

Top centre: Country and western singer Porter Wagoner in 1979 – quintessential Rhinestone Cowboy.

Top right: Matchbox, on stage at the Music Machine (now the Camden Palace), London, 1979. Photo: David Corio.

Above: 'Authentic' Western-style outfit available by mail order, 1952.

Left: Fans suitably dressed for the Wembley Country Music Festival, London, 1986. Photo: David Corio.

Fashion designers have long looked to Western Style for inspiration.
Right: Gold chaps featured in Jean-Paul Gaultier's Spring/Summer 1993 collection.

Below: From Gianni Versace's Autumn/Winter 1992/93 collection.
Photos: Niall McInerney.

strippers (hence the nickname) but he eventually opened a shop in Los Angeles from which he supplied increasingly ostentatious creations to the likes of Gene Autry, Roy Rogers, Porter Wagoner and Elvis Presley, and, more recently, to Dolly Parton, Elton John and others. For Nudie there was no such thing as too much embroidery or too much glitter.

Did Nudie single-handedly destroy country and western's claim to down-home simplicity and authenticity? Certainly, for those of us who are not fans of Nashville-type country and western music it is easy to mock the Rhinestone Cowboy's OTT, ostentatious image. Yet we would probably hesitate to sneer at Cab Calloway's equally OTT Zootie style. And in fact both address the same need: the need felt by those who come from poor backgrounds to use their personal style as a badge of success. In its way, a Nudie suit dripping with rhinestones symbolized triumph over adversity just as much as Cab Calloway's zoot suit or the more restrained costume of the original 'singing cowboys'.

bikers

'Whaddya rebellin' against, Johnny?'

On the Fourth of July weekend, 1947, motorcycle races were held in the town of Hollister, California. Things got out of hand when some of the men attending this event ('1 percent', according to the organizers) staged drag races down the main street, started drunken brawls, made crude advances to local women and looted bars. A journalist called Frank Rooney wrote about the incident in the *Saturday Evening Post* and his article was picked up by the film producer Stanley Kramer who in 1954 turned it into a film starring Marlon Brando called *The Wild One*. The rest is history.

'Whaddya rebellin' against, Johnny?'
'Wha' ya got?'
But who were the real-life models of Brando's 'Johnny'?

Apparently many of them were servicemen recently returned from the war who found it difficult adapting to life in post-war America, an America which was undergoing remarkably rapid social changes as it adjusted to peacetime. The booming television and advertising industries were fostering 'a vision of a whole nation sharing a standard suit and a standard haircut, a standard home equipped with the standard appliances, standard car, kids and dog'.[1]

Today we might take such standardization as part and parcel of modern life, but for those with their adrenalin still flowing from the life-and-death excitement of war, such bland conformity was hard to accept. As Mick Farren puts it:

There was a percentage of men returning

He's got the bike, he's got the 'Perfecto' and he's got the girl.
How come he's still not satisfied? Marlon Brando
in *The Wild One*, 1954.

from the wars in both Europe and the Pacific who couldn't find it in themselves to go along with the welcome home, pacification programme. It's hard to settle to bagging in a supermarket after you've been the waist gunner in a B17.[2]

Instead of planes, many of these men turned to motorbikes. But mode of transport was only the symbolic focus for a lifestyle that was radically different from anything that had come before. Clustered in tightly knit gangs with names like 'The Booze Fighters' (precursors of the 'Hells Angels'), these early postwar Bikers set out to challenge every aspect of the New American Way. And they succeeded (thanks in part to Kramer and Brando).

Central to this success was their distinctive style. Whereas, as we have seen, the classic sartorial response of working-class people is to dress up in rich styles in order to 'ape their betters', the Bikers defied stylistic as well as other conventions by proudly presenting themselves in rugged working-class garments. Finery was not their way – they preferred rough-and-ready, battered clothes which visually demonstrated their harsh experiences on the road.

Of course the war had served to elevate the status of certain garments – most noticeably the black leather jacket. Whereas in earlier wars the military elite had appeared in formal attire embellished with gold braid, the Second World War saw the likes of Patton and MacArthur wearing precisely the same black leather jackets that the Bikers now took as their uniform. But, as the Bikers' appearance grew steadily more scruffy and frayed (Brando's costume was far too immaculate), this association with heroism was deliberately undermined.

These were *outlaws* living beyond social convention. 'Born To Lose' desperadoes who scoffed at the very possibility of making it

within society, the Bikers of the late 1940s and early 1950s represented a radical departure from previous motorcycling subcultures and, obviously, from mainstream society. Both stylistically and ideologically (the two, of course, always amounting to the same thing in the end) they were outsiders with no interest in becoming insiders.

Although the Zooties and the Rhinestone Cowboys can hardly be said to have occupied centre stage in 'normal society', their dress did demonstrate the fact that their ultimate aspirations subscribed to mainstream definitions of The Good Life. The same cannot be said of the Biker.

Yet his (and occasionally her) approach to life has been the one which has perhaps most tellingly changed the course of contemporary

history. Just as the black leather jacket has become an acceptable streetstyle (even high fashion) garment, so too have we all come to question that boring, cosy normality against which the Bikers rebelled. It's arguable that the Bikers, more dramatically and vividly than any other subculture, kick-started those notions of *alternativeness* and *badness* which have become such key motifs of both streetstyle and rock/pop music.

'Wha' ya got?'

Well, Johnny, what we've got is an interesting irony. In the decades since you cruised into town on your Triumph, the local townsfolk have taken to dressing and acting like you. Everyone's got a black leather jacket and a Bad Attitude to go with it. Now we're all just a bunch of no good punks.

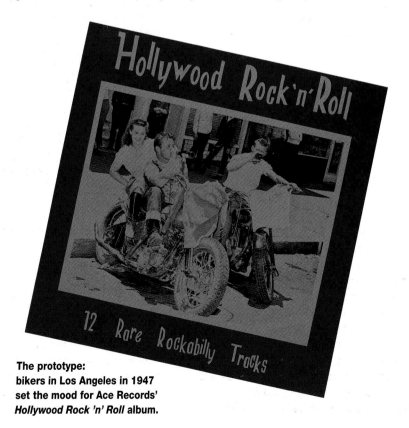

The prototype: bikers in Los Angeles in 1947 set the mood for Ace Records' *Hollywood Rock 'n' Roll* album.

When musical styles change, so do dress styles. (Or is it the other way round?) The zoot-suited jazzmen of the late 1930s and early 1940s played 'swing', which (though sometimes incorporating hip, jive elements) was always a highly orchestrated, rich, luxurious music. Like the zoot suit it was most at home in a swanky nightclub.

Later in the forties, after the war, a new, experimental and strangely innovative music began to emerge. Called 'bebop', its natural habitat was the smaller jazz clubs of New York City. Uptown in Harlem there was Minton's Playhouse (where, it is said, bebop was born). Later, downtown on 52nd Street, there were the Three Deuces, the Onyx, the Downbeat Club and Kelly's Stable. Instead of a full orchestra, bebop required only a handful of musicians, a set-up that was ideal for the improvisation and experimentation which lay at the heart of this new music.

To most ears the sounds produced were alien, atonal and without structure, but to musicians like Charlie Parker, Thelonious Monk and Dizzy Gillespie, bebop was the sweet sound of jazz finally breaking free. Swing had been extrovert and dance-oriented, bebop was geared for more mental perambulations. These were not jive-ass entertainers but deadly serious musicians. And, as such, they required a new visual style.

Over the next few years this dress style would steadily emerge, and the key to it was eccentricity. Consider a famous early photograph of Thelonious Monk and his fellow band members standing outside Minton's Playhouse (*above left*). All four wear double-breasted suits which are roomy by today's standards (though skintight compared to the zoot suit). But check out the accessories. As well as a tie, Monk wears a scarf tied around his neck, really cosmic hi-tech shades and, to top it all off, a black beret. While Cab Calloway's clothes proclaimed, 'I've got it made,' Monk's

hip cats & hipsters

Opposite: Thelonius Monk, Howard McGhee, Roy Eldridge and Teddy Hill outside Minton's Playhouse, Harlem, 1950s.

Above: Dig it! Dizzie Gillespie shows off a leopardskin jacket and other groovie Hipster threads from Fox Brothers of Chicago, a firm which outfitted practically everyone on the jazz scene through the 1940s and into the 1950s .

Right: Bebop Hipsters hit the streets of San Francisco circa 1949. Illustration: Chris Sullivan.

proclaim, 'I'm one of a kind' – or, in the parlance of the day, 'I'm one hip cat.'

Like bebop the music, bebop the style operated according to its own rules – outside the system. Although Charlie Parker never excelled stylistically (presumably he had other things on his mind), Monk and Gillespie proved themselves to be innovators in both media. In particular, their goatee beards, shades and extraordinarily wide and eclectic range of headgear defined a look which would be as widely imitated as their music. Their sartorial disciples (who survive even today in Acid Jazz) were known as 'Hipsters'.

The origins and meaning of this word are as difficult to pin down as its ramifications are difficult to exaggerate. Historically, the term 'Hipster' has come to be identified with the 1950s and with bebop, but Cab Calloway wrote and published a *Hipster's Dictionary* as far back as 1938. And, as we have already seen, Malcolm X used the term to describe himself and his zoot-suited comrades in the early forties.

Whereas in this earlier period the Hipster was black (Calloway, Malcolm X), by the late forties he seems to have become (in Norman Mailer's phrase) 'a white negro'. And whereas the original Black Hipster had been locked out of mainstream white society by virtue of his colour, the White Hipster locked himself out and threw away the key. At its heart,

therefore, hipsterness was a rejection of the 'straight' lifestyle and (as Mick Farren asserts in *The Black Leather Jacket* [1]) it pervaded and defined a wide range of late 1940s/1950s subcultures – the Bikers and the Beats as well as the beboppers. (Brando once described *The Wild One* as a portrayal of 'hipster psychology'. The indebtedness of the Beats – and later the Hippies – to this attitude is obvious.)

But stylistically the Hipsters were a more specific phenomenon. Their berets, shades and goatees all pointed directly back to those bebop innovators like Dizzy and Monk who gave the world both a look and a music of lasting importance.

hip cats & hipsters   **29**

The real thing. Neal Cassady and Jack Kerouac in no-nonsense Beat style. San Francisco, 1952. Photo: Carolyn Cassady.

On the Road, Jack Kerouac's Beat classic, is a resumé of the streetstyle story so far. It has Hipsters, Beboppers, Bikers, Pachucos, Zooties and even a character who is said to resemble Gene Autry. In the midst of all this sharp style stride Dean Moriarty and Sal Paradise, kitted out in studied indifference – a sort of sartorial degree zero. Anti-style for anti-heroes.

Consider Carolyn Cassady's photograph of Neal Cassady and Jack Kerouac, the prototypes for Moriarty and Paradise, which appears on the cover of the most recent Penguin edition of On the Road. Neal Cassady wears a pale, crumpled workshirt and what looks like a fairly new pair of 501s. Jack Kerouac (looking every inch the collegiate athlete he once was) wears a light coloured sweatshirt and a pair of chinos. That's it. And nor do their rather nondescript hairstyles suggest the makings of a revolution.

Of course the very fact that these two look so 'normal' is a tribute to their stylistic as well as literary impact. Those of us who today wear workshirts, sweatshirts and jeans (and who do not own an iron) do so in part because of a tradition of sartorial nonchalance which the Beats began.

Yet there are two fascinating ironies here. The first hinges on the fact that this seeming lack of interest in appearance and dress (On the Road Dean suddenly asks, 'Now what's the sense of clothes?' and everyone strips off) occurs within a milieu of sartorial obsession.

When our heroes meet up with the Great-orooni jazz musician Slim Gaillard (identified by Dean as 'God') we are not told what Slim is wearing but I think we can be sure that he wasn't dressed in scruffy anti-style. The same could be said of the Hipsters, the Zooties and even the lone Biker who roars past 'all bespangled and bedecked with glittering buttons, visor, slick black jacket, a Texas poet of the night'.[1] Everything else about

beats & beatniks & existentialists

these characters is an inspiration for Moriarty and Paradise – their jazz, their drugs, their free-wheeling passion . . . everything except their clothing fetishism.

This fact is especially important in drawing a line between the Beat and the White Hipster (who are often, erroneously, seen as one and the same). While the Hipster fusses and preens to get the look just right, the Beat scoffs (at least publicly) at such materialistic narcissism. But perhaps this is just the point. The Hipster wants in – he truly does want 'to make the scene'. The Beat, however, is just passing through, an anthropologist of the underworld, and he signals his alienness not by presenting an alternative style but rather by an indifference (conscious though it may be) to style itself. None of which would be so remarkable were it not for the fact that the world which the Beat chooses to pass through is a world where style is deified.

Another irony. These original members of the Beat Generation don't even look like Beats. Like Cassady and Kerouac in their photographs, Dean Moriarty and Sal Paradise don't seem actually to own any *black* garments. Nor do they wear goatees, sandals or berets. So where then did 'Beat Style' come from?

Perhaps the answer lies not in Greenwich Village or in San Francisco, but in Paris, on the Left Bank. While history has no doubt exaggerated, it seems clear that the Existentialists did subscribe to Henry Ford's dictum, 'Any colour so long as it is black'. Juliette Greco in black polo-neck, black trousers and heavy black eyeliner does seem to be a genuine perpetrator of a style which would be forever associated with the Beats.

And though Paris seems a long way from New York, let us bear in mind that from the late forties those jazz musicians whom the Beats revered were regularly travelling to Paris to perform. On one such trip Miles Davis

met and fell in love with Juliette Greco, who introduced him to Sartre and the other Existentialists. Looking at the photograph which appears on the cover of Davis's autobiography – in which he is dressed completely in black – one cannot help but imagine him with Greco and Sartre in Saint Germain. Broadening the picture to take in more traditional French garments like the beret and the striped Breton shirt (as worn by Picasso) one could hypothesize that the core of what became known as 'Beat Style' was actually Left-Bank style as seen through the dark shades of American jazz musicians.

But even if such speculation is correct, it is still a long way from Le Tabou or even Birdland to that image of the Beatnik which has become such an icon of hip rebellion. The reason for this is simple: it is a long way from the Beat to the Beatnik. The latter, rather than evolving naturally from the original Beat Generation (who hated the term 'Beatnik',

Above: Beatnik self-caricature, as seen on the walls of Eel Pie Island jazz club, London, 1961.

Left: San Francisco 'bohemians' in the 1960 film *The Subterraneans*, which was loosely based on the novel of the same name by Jack Kerouac.

Right: *Through Beatnik Eyeballs*, a 'picture of teenage society that may shock many adults', was published in 1961. Its 'Glossary for Squares' included everything from 'Beatsville' and 'Blast' to 'Zootie'.

Far right: The real Beat look by mail, 1960.

Below: US fashion designer Ralph Lauren chose to draw upon Beatnik/Existentialist influences for his Spring/Summer 1993 collection. Photo: Niall McInerney.

with good reason) was created by journalists, who used it as a term of abuse.[2] From this point on, a caricatured stereotype would overshadow the original, genuine article.

This is always the way in streetstyle. Be it Beats, Rockers, Punks or Ravers, we end up with a mental image which bears little resemblance to its original inspiration. In the case of the Beat/Beatnik, however, the gap between prototype and assembly-line product seems particularly mind-boggling.

Out of the Beats' deadly earnest search for a 'new vision' came a figure of fun, a clown. The 1959 British film *Expresso Bongo* featured whole coffee bars full of them. But it was the American television sitcom *The Many Loves of Dobie Gillis* which took this caricature to its apotheosis. While Dobie Gillis was the lovable, squeaky clean vision of suburban normality, his neighbour Maynard G. Krebs came complete with goatee, oversized black sweaters, sandals, hip-speak and bongos. A sort of precursor of the Fonz of *Happy Days*, Maynard G. Krebs (unlike the Fonz) never graduated from figure of fun to hero. It is, in other words, hard to see this Beatnik clown as anything but a comic assassin of the original Beat creation.

And yet another slant might be put on this bit of pop culture trivia. I was a young teenager growing up in suburban America

when *Dobie Gillis* first appeared on television. Like the rest of the family I thought Maynard G. Krebs was a joke but I can recall that the thought also crept into my head that, given the choice, I would rather be in his sandals than in Dobie Gillis's boring footwear. Within a year or so I had read both *On the Road* and *Howl*. And I also discovered the delights of progressive jazz.

Streetstyle depends on the media to make isolated pockets of stylistic and ideological innovation accessible to those who (like myself in my youth) live beyond the geography of 'Where It's At'. Whether intentional or not, whether malicious or good-humoured, the media's interpretation of The Real Thing is inevitably stereotyped and distorted. Nevertheless, a reading-between-the-lines deconstruction of this fiction is always possible – working backwards to hypothesize a true point of origin. In this way tiny cliques are transformed into international styletribes and the creative spark of a few becomes part of a generalized history which shapes all our lives. Maynard G. Krebs may have been no Cassady or Kerouac, but he too played a part in that Beat Revolution which forced a critical appraisal of a way of life grown increasingly conformist, standardized, shallow and just plain 'square'.

For their 1954 article 'The Truth about the "Teddy Boy"', *Picture Post* plucked this regular from the Mecca Dance Hall in Tottenham, London, to show off his classic 'Edwardian' style.

While postwar USA was focused on the pros and cons of its new consumer society, in Britain the ration book's continued presence into the early 1950s fostered other concerns. Throughout the long years of the war everyone in the UK had been admonished to pull together for the common good. Now that peace had come, there was an expectation on the part of the British working class that shared hardship would be rewarded with a more classless and egalitarian society. The most immediate and obvious consequence of this expectation was the election of a Labour government. But there were also more subtle manifestations and inevitably these would come to include that most sensitive barometer of social change – appearance style.

Soon after the war, the tailors of Savile Row – the traditional, typically conservative arbiters of British upper-class, male dress style – produced a more flamboyant line of menswear which came to be known as 'Edwardian' because it harked back to the golden age of Edward VII. Jackets in this style were single-breasted, long, fitted and often featured velvet trim on the collar or cuffs. They were worn with narrow trousers and fancy brocade waistcoats. Britain as a nation needed to regain pride in itself and this upper-class 'Edwardian' style served both to symbolize a time when the greatness of Britain had been beyond dispute and to put a check on the ever increasing cultural hegemony of America.

Well and good. But from the perspective of the British working classes another interpretation must have been all too evident. The promise of a more egalitarian and less class-ridden society was being mocked by these upper-class 'toffs' in their velvet-trimmed collars and fancy accessories who were emphasizing rather than eradicating the demarcation line between the privileged and

teddy boys

Left: A later, more stereotyped, Teddy Boy look displayed at the seafront at Lowestoft, Suffolk, 1962.

Below: Reissue brothel creepers. This ad appeared in 1978, during the Teddy Boy revival of that period.

Opposite: Teddy Boy family in Dublin, 1985. Photo: Steve Pyke.

the 'lower orders'. So much for everyone pulling together.

This might have been the end of the story – game, set and match to the toffs – were it not for the fact that another social revolution was in the making. Whereas in the past childhood had jolted suddenly into adulthood, increasingly an intermediate status – The Teenager – was coming into being. The driving force behind this new identity came from the world of advertising and marketing, where note had been taken of the increased numbers and spending power of adolescents. But, once unleashed, *The Teenager* became a sort of Frankenstein's monster which could not be subdued – reaching out far beyond its own demographic territory to leave its mark on almost every aspect of Western culture.

This mix of working-class aspirations and youthful assertiveness created a powerful cocktail. Its effect, in retrospect, should have

been predictable but few commentators seem to have seen it coming. Early in 1952, in solidly working-class parts of London like the Elephant & Castle – south of the Thames and bleak by anyone's standards – young men started dressing up in a style which took the upper-class 'Edwardian' look and added to it eclectic features of American origin – Zootie styling and the cowboy's 'maverick' tie.

It was a bizarre mix but somehow it all worked aesthetically, lending an aura of dignity, grace and elegance to young men whose fathers had gone through life flat cap in hand, stylistically inhibited, knowing their place. The gauntlet had been thrown down. The 'New Edwardians', as they came to be known, were cashing in the I.O.U. that their class had been begrudgingly offered during the most dire days of the war – the promise that come the victory everyone would be invited to the ball.

Needless to say the powers that be were not pleased. At first the media treated these 'New Edwardians' or 'Teddy Boys' as a joke, but the strategy soon switched to that of questioning their masculinity. Psychologists were hauled out to explain how the absence of the Teddy Boys' fathers during the war had derailed their normal development. The Teds fought words with images. They might preen and strut like peacocks but their macho demeanour left no one in doubt that these were 100 percent male peacocks.

Contrary to historical glossing, all this was going on prior to rock 'n' roll's invasion of Britain. It was the big bands who supplied the soundtrack in the early days (with the likes of Ted Heath and Ken Mackintosh creating songs especially aimed at the New Edwardians). But when Bill Haley's *Rock around the Clock* and the hit songs of the likes of Elvis Presley and Jerry Lee Lewis did

TOO YOUNG TO DIE

DRAPE JACKETS
Same as shown. Finger length, two button style, velvet collar, two side pockets, half moon cuffs, top pockets and bar. Colour of jacket either blac.. or blue, colour of velvet black, blue, yellow or red. State choice of jacket colour and velvet trims. When ordering state chest size and under arm to finger length measurement.

£25.00 includes P&P

bootlace ties
Available in cow-head, pistol and holster or horse motif. AMERICAN IMPORT.

75p - 5p P&P

rams head belt
Imported from Greece. All leather. TREMENDOUSLY HEAVY HEAD.

£3.50 includes P&P

drainpipe jeans
13" bottoms. Tight fitting. Only in Denim. Sizes 28-36.

£3.00 includes P&P

brothel creepers
Thick 2" black microsole. Specially designed for boppin' and jivin'. Available in jive black or rocking blue. Sizes 6-11.

Only **£7.99** includes P&P

FREE Catalogue of "TOO YOUNG TO DIE" extensive range of rock fashions, sent free on request.

ORPHEUS (Dept. NME)
THE TRICORN
PORTSMOUTH, HANTS.

Members of The Edwardian Drape Society (T.E.D.S.) keep the original style alive at a 1993 get-together in London.

Above right: **The complete Teddy Boy look – velvet-trimmed drape, bootlace tie, ram's-head belt, drainpipes and brothel creepers – available through the small ads in the music press, late 1970s.**

cross the Atlantic in 1956, a marriage was made in heaven.

Even if, from an American perspective, it was all most confusing. The Teddy Boys' uniform didn't remotely resemble the American vision of rock 'n' roll and when Bill Haley and others visited Britain they were flummoxed by what they saw. I was too, when, as an American living in London, I happened to drop in to a rock 'n' roll get-together at London's Alexandra Palace in 1972. Nothing equivalent to this look – or this style of dancing – ever existed in the USA.

If the pre-rock 'n' roll New Edwardians had been seen as threatening to the status quo, the post-rock 'n' roll Teddy Boy – armed with a style that was increasingly his own and with the thrusting power of this alien new music – was positively dangerous. What sociologists term a 'moral panic' set in, fuelled on the one hand by an increasingly hysterical media and on the other by the Ted's own willingness to act the part of the hooligan. Slashed cinema seats, flick knives in the back pocket next to the obligatory greasy comb and alleged participation in the Notting Hill race riots all helped to make the

64-PAGE THRILLING DETECTIVE NOVEL

The TEDDY-BOY MYSTERY
by John Drummond

THE SEXTON BLAKE LIBRARY 9d No 334

Left: *The Teddy Boy Mystery,* by John Drummond, in which a group of 'tearaways' prove themselves to be good old-fashioned salt-of-the-earth Brits under their Edwardian garb.

Below: The long lines of the classic Teddy Boy drape jacket made an appearance in Katharine Hamnett's Autumn/Winter 1990 collection. Photo: Niall McInerney.

term Teddy Boy synonymous with juvenile delinquent.

Throughout the fifties and well into the sixties any kid who got into trouble – whatever his style or lack of it – would be classified as a 'Ted'. Only in the early 1970s, when a rock 'n' roll revival was broadly seen as quaint nostalgia for a time prior to the drug-taking Hippies and the aggressive Skinheads, did this begin to change. This PR transformation was given a further boost in the late 1970s with the emergence of Punk, and when this bizarre new life form clashed with the Teds in well publicized battles on the King's Road, the prevalent media view saw the Teds as comforting time-travellers from an altogether saner and safer era.

It has been said that the Teds were 'the first to walk down that road to the promised land of Teen Age'.[1] At first glance this seems like hyperbole (or perhaps simply a too exclusively British approach). What about the young Malcolm X and his friends cutting out in their zoot suits? What about the Zazous? The Bikers? The Hipsters? The Beats? True, many were too old to qualify as teenagers, but many were well within the magic age range.

But they would not have seen themselves as 'teens' for the simple reason that this classification had yet to be invented. The Teddy Boys knew that they were boys – not yet fully fledged, chained-down-by-job-and-family men – and this both energized their rebellion and defined its nature. Stylistically they have become (indeed, in a sense, always were) anachronisms, but the Teddy Boys' existence as a subculture celebrated and reflected a modern social environment which could not have existed prior to the Second World War. Even at the start of the war it is hard to imagine anyone taking seriously the prospect of so many young people refusing to defer to the wisdom of age, or of the 'lower orders' refusing to defer to their 'betters'. Secretive mutters under the breath, perhaps, but the bold proclamation of such things in one's dress, on the street, was quite another matter.

In an international context this distinctive, uniquely British look was hardly known, let alone imitated. But the Teddy Boys set the stage for many generations of British youth-culture and streetstyle which would grab the world by the short 'n' curlies and not let go.

modernists

The twentieth century divides neatly between a *hot* half and a *cool* half. This had nothing to do with the weather and everything to do with a shift in the cultural climate. While the ramifications of this change in attitude and demeanour extend throughout every facet of Western culture, the birth of the cool – like the birth of the hot – derives from jazz. As Joe Goldberg put it so eloquently in his essay in *A Catalog of Cool*:

The A Train departs. The world awaits a new lick. Years later, everyone else will find a way to put their own spin to the word 'cool'. Cool this, cool that. But when it first arrives on a subterranean rail headed for the heart of Bop City, it belongs to jazz alone.[1]

In the late 1940s *avant-garde* jazz musicians were determined to distance themselves from the way in which their musical tradition had been usurped by mainstream, white society. The standardized suburban lifestyle, which we have already considered, blithely embraced the likes of Louis Armstrong and His Hot Five, so that musicians concerned with overturning Armstrong's primacy couldn't call themselves '"hot" no matter how blazing they were'.[2] The only thing for it was to reduce the temperature.

The first moves in this direction were made within bebop. In 1947 Charlie Parker recorded 'Cool Blues' while Dizzy Gillespie recorded 'Cool Breeze'. But bebop – especially in its trend towards 'hard bop' and the Latin-inspired 'cubop' – would always be too intense, too hot to handle within this meteorological framework. The true 'Cool School', as it came to be known, was conceived in a little apartment on West 55th Street, New York, where the Canadian-born (white) arranger Gil Evans was host to a small coterie of musicians including John Lewis (who would go on to form the Modern Jazz Quartet), the white saxophonist Gerry Mulligan and a young trumpet player from St Louis named Miles Davis.

'Kind of Blue' – Cool School Modernist vibe of the late 1950s. Illustration: Chris Sullivan.

Opposite: Latin Cool School – Machito's rhythm section, performing in the late 1940s, kitted out in slimline, collarless jackets.

Right: The Modern Jazz Quartet in 1953, wearing the minimal style which suited their music so perfectly. Photo: William Claxton.

The music which would grow from these get-togethers broke with long-established jazz conventions. As Richard Williams describes it in *Miles Davis: The Man in the Green Shirt*:

Jazz, since its early days on the streets of New Orleans, had been a music with a strong component of competitive machismo . . . Indeed, faster, higher, stronger could have been a motto for virtually all trumpeters before Miles Davis, all arrangers before Gil Evans. But these two were hearing something different: a music with deeper currents and softer, subtler colours, the product of a sensibility formed by factors other than strength and endurance.[3]

The result of which was *Birth of the Cool*, which was recorded in 1949 and 1950: a line drawn between the two halves of the century.

What was cool was also *modern* and it is here that this new music fuses with a visual aesthetic which had been around in architecture and design at least since the Bauhaus movement of the 1920s but which only really made an impact on popular culture around the time that Miles Davis *et al* were recording *Birth of the Cool*. Modern was /is sleek, sharp and minimal. In other words, the visual equivalent of the new jazz. The Cool School would have to get some new suits.

The Modernist Style marks the apex of the pendulum's swing away from the zoot suit. The beboppers had been moving and grooving in the right direction but their double-breasted, padded-shoulder suits would have to go. It didn't happen overnight but slowly and surely everything became slimmer and trimmer, less ornate. Cool, modern, sharp – call it what you will, it all came down to the same thing: Less Is More.

Joe Goldberg describes the shock of the new in *A Catalogue of Cool*:

There were several stores along Broadway displaying these wonders. The hippest of them all but, sadly, a world I never made, was Phil Kronfeld. In the conformist Fifties, Phil Kronfeld used to show a suit in his window that looked like a Lenny Bruce parody of the regimental banker's gray flannel. It was gray, all right, but not the dark Wall Street-shadowed gray. It was a light gray, as light as your mother's hair, and it was single-breasted, in a time when double-breasteds were still the thing. Most outrageous of all, it only had one button. One button! Do you understand what that means? Can you visualize how deep the cleavage went, how much of your solid-knot tie it showed?[4]

The Cool School look circa 1950 was rooted in Hipster style. Even if the essential suit had gone from double to singlebreasted, had slimmed down considerably – even, in some cases, dispensing with a collar altogether and thereby beating out Cardin by a decade – it was still too flash and fussy to qualify as 100 percent Modernist. The cuffs and cufflinks would have to go. The shirt collar would have to lose its flamboyant points and get buttoned down in Ivy League style. Most importantly, the tie would have to become a line as thin and sharp as on a Mondrian. Not pointed at the bottom, but cut off square and held down by a very discreet tie clip worn three-quarters of the way down.

It would take a while for this look to percolate through, but the temperature was dropping fast. By mid-decade the coolest of the cool had shunned all that was ostentatious in favour of the progressive, the minimal and the modern. This was the sound of *Kind of Blue* and the Modern Jazz Quartet but, ironically, the look that went with it – the definitive Modernist look – would be perfected not by a jazz musician but by Malcolm X – a man who would no doubt hate to be remembered for his dress sense, but nevertheless a man who managed to epitomize both hot and cool styles: original Zootie and minimal Modernist.

folkies

Like the Beats, the Folkies can be seen as a reaction against the standardized and bland 'consumer society' which increasingly characterized North America and Northern Europe in the 1950s. For this reason the media has often tended to lump these two subcultures together. But though the Beats and the Folkies had much in common, they also possessed distinctive characteristics which are important because they set out alternative paths within the history of streetstyle.

While the Beats, the Beatniks and the Left-Bank Existentialists were musically grounded in modern jazz, the Folkies – as their name suggests – looked for inspiration to the folk music traditions of rural communities. Such musical preferences give a clue to a more fundamental, ideological difference. The modern jazz which the Beats took as the soundtrack of their lifestyle was profoundly urban in character. Even if the likes of Kerouac were happy to go *On the Road*, their ultimate destination (both actual and mythical) was the urban jungle.

As was the case with the Beats, the Folkies typically lived in cities and suburbs but their hearts – like their soundtrack – were rooted in the country. This yearning for rural simplicity is reminiscent of the same forces which in the 1930s and 1940s led many a city dweller to hanker after the image of the Western Cowboy. But while the country-and-western scene would gradually develop a more aspirational image in the form of the Rhinestone Cowboy, the Folkies (usually middle-class and educationally privileged) would crave a purer and in theory more authentic rural lifestyle. (In a sense, that rural poverty which the Rhinestone Cowboy was eager to leave behind was also that rural idyll

which the Folkies dreamed of from a very different sociological perspective.)

This identification with old-fashioned, traditional rural life pointed the Folkies in a different direction from that of the Beats. Inclined towards celebrating the human spirit, and ultimately optimistic, the Folkies could not share the Beats' nihilism. And out of their optimism came a tendency towards political activism. While the Beats despaired of the human condition, the Folkies were convinced that something could be done about it.

All of which, needless to say, found stylistic expression in dress. The Folkies favoured brighter colours and decoration. A decade later this would eventually flower (literally) into the ethnically inspired, often embroidered styles of the Hippies.

Sitting in a folk club in Greenwich Village or London's Soho in the late fifties or early sixties, you might have noticed oversized, 'Sloppy Joe' sweaters in colours other than the ubiquitous black of the nearby jazz clubs. You might have seen men in corduroy trousers or corduroy jackets and women in subtle flower-print skirts or blouses. From these tentative beginnings would evolve a style which, like the music, spoke of pre-industrial rural life – the emphasis on natural fabrics and colours, the use of hand-crafted embroidery, an earthy rusticity in total contrast to that futuristic modernism which was so characteristic of the 1950s.

In terms of aesthetics and attitude, it is but a short step from here to Woodstock and Glastonbury.

Folkie dress styles in evidence at a performance of the Skiffle Gypsies in Brighton, late 1950s.

rockabillies

Classic, casual yet elegant Rockabilly style, as shown on Ace Records' compilation *The Best of Rockabilly*, 1981.

Black 'rock' from rhythm and blues hitched up with the 'billy' of the hillbillies

Memphis, Tennessee, is neither here nor there. It's not actually part of the 'Deep South' but neither is it Western, Eastern or Northern. Perhaps it is this geographic and cultural indeterminacy which accounts for its ability to spark a fusion of musical and stylistic influences which were so diverse – even contradictory – that they were bound to change history.

In 1954 a truck driver called Elvis Presley sang a few songs for Sun Records boss Sam Phillips and the rest, as they say, is history. So much so that it is almost impossible for us today to appreciate just how revolutionary all this was. They called Presley 'The Hillbilly Cat' and herein lies an important clue. The 'hillbilly' reference spoke of a poor, white, Southern heritage which had belligerently insulated itself from the 'negro' culture flowering all around it. But the 'cat' reference linked this young musician directly to the 'Hip Cats' of the black jazz tradition.

In a sense Presley and those who followed in his wake, like Jerry Lee Lewis or Carl Perkins, were Hipsters – 'with it', sharp-dressing white guys who picked up on (some would say stole) black influences. Previously, however, the standard issue Hipster had been a white *Northerner*. For such interracial cultural inbreeding to be taking place south of the Mason-Dixon Line was nothing short of extraordinary.

While the typical white Hipster lurking around Times Square had taken on the styles of black jazzmen lock-stock-and-barrel right down to the beret and beard, these southern Hipsters – these Rockabillies – retained too much of their own cultural heritage to fit within Norman Mailer's definition of the Hipster as 'white negro'. These were 'good old boys' (and occasionally 'good old girls')

who retained much of their musical and stylistic traditions while reaching out to contemporary black culture. In short, Rockabilly was a marriage of separate and distinct elements. (Even if, from a black perspective, it was a marriage for which no consent had ever been given.) Black 'rock' from rhythm and blues hitched up with the 'billy' of the hillbillies.

Needless to say, a great many important historical transformations had to occur before such an unlikely coupling could take place. The Second World War had brought people from all over the USA into direct contact with each other. Likewise, migration from rural to urban areas (as in Presley's own experience) brought a new intimacy between culturally disparate peoples. This was further encouraged by the proliferation of local radio stations across America (which meant, for example, that the young Elvis could listen to the latest R&B releases) and the emergence of the national television networks. No longer could Americans of any race or cultural background live in isolation and ignorance of other lifestyles.

Yet all of this probably pales into insignificance when we take one further social transformation into account – the birth of the teenager. In 1955, when the twenty-year-old Elvis was first demonstrating how he could turn his female fans to jelly with his pelvic gyrations, James Dean's teen classic *Rebel without a Cause* was playing to packed audiences across America.

Although Presley and Dean were not themselves 'baby boomers', their young fans were. This huge demographic bulge represented far too great a consumer group to be ignored. Almost overnight, 'youth' became *the* key component of personal

Left: Original Rockabilly style as worn by the Polecats' guitarist, Boz. Photographed backstage at the Marquee club in London in 1981 by David Corio.

Right: Cruising on the London 'Rockin' Scene' in 1990. Photo: Vanessa Bell.

Far right: The rough-and-ready 'Dirtbox look' on London's King's Road, early 1980s.

identity – reducing the importance of other, previously absolute divisions and defining 'teenagers' as an almost homogeneous culture in their own right.

The barriers of ethnic or regional background and, of course, race, were still there but for many members of this new generation their importance was overshadowed by the increasing significance of 'the age barrier'. The kinds of fusion which Rockabilly represented were a thousand times more likely within this new, revolutionary teen world where the real division between 'us' and 'them' was age.

The musical components of Rockabilly's extraordinary interracial fusion are readily discernible, with the black traditions of rhythm and blues, gospel and jazz distinguished from the white traditions of country and western. However, the roots of Rockabilly's distinctive appearance style are less readily identifiable, partly because the debt which Rockabilly style owes to black influences is one of general tone rather than of specific features of dress.

Whereas the Hipster simply wore copies of styles which had been devised by black jazzmen, the Rockabilly took the general principle that men could proudly strut the world's stage as peacocks and reworked this within the already established tradition of the white, Southern dandy. Specific features of this look included a liberal use of white and pastel coloured fabrics and generous quantities of decoration (including diamond-

shaped designs, piping, embroidery, visible stitching, added blocks of colour, inset seams in vivid, contrasting colours and extra-wide shirt collars worn over the jacket lapels). Trousers tended to be 'pegged' – roomy at the top but reduced to a minimum at the ankle. And then the shoes: snow white, contrasting two-tone or, in the words of the Carl Perkins song, blue suede.

All of which is clearly in the Dressing Up tradition already seen in both Zooties and Western Style. Certainly, the Rockabillies of Memphis and elsewhere fit socio-economically within the pattern: they were poor kids using their attire to demand respect and to demonstrate success – their pristine, immaculate style proclaiming a life unsullied by manual labour.

And yet Rockabilly, perhaps uniquely, also generated a completely opposite look. By 1957 Elvis would appear on film wearing a well-worn denim work jacket, jeans and boots. The contrast with his sleek white suit and spotless white shoes of 1956 is absolute. But somehow this was appropriate and logical: having demonstrated that he was no longer a truck driver he is free to remind us of his roots.

In Britain, two decades later, both Rockabilly styles would be revived and revered. In 1976 (the same year as Punk) a few keyplayers in London's rock 'n' roll scene swapped their Teddy Boy drapes for worn denim dungarees and even clay pipes in emulation of that American 'hillbilly' style

personified by Li'l Abner in the comic strip. When the Teds condemned the scruffiness of this style (and its complete disregard of the 'Ted hierarchy'), the rock 'n' roll scene split into two irreconcilable factions. From these few 'hillbillies' grew a huge youth subculture which sought to escape from Britain's problems (the lack of work and hope summarized by the Punks in their famous 'No Future' slogan) by immersing themselves in all manner of fifties-style Americana.

At the sharp end of this movement was a British Rockabilly revival which modelled itself with religious fervour on that flashy but cleancut style which had been epitomized by Elvis in 1956. These new Rockabillies bought such items as 'pink peg slacks' (in the words of the Eddie Cochran song) from little shops like Rock-a-Cha in Kensington Market and danced the night away in clubs like the Royalty in Southgate and the Squire in Catford.

In 1985, however, the place-to-be was the 'Dirtbox' and, as its name suggests, the predominant style had shifted from immaculate suits and white shoes to denim jackets and jeans so worn and frayed that only sweat seemed to keep them from falling off. Like Elvis, these British Rockabillies had gone from one stylistic extreme to the other in the blink of an eye.

Such contrariness is unusual if not unique in the history of streetstyle: Dressing Up and Dressing Down logically serving as either/or rather than multiple-choice options. But then Rockabilly was born of contradiction (the collision of black and southern white cultures) and perhaps it is simply in its nature to indulge in the unexpected. Perhaps, too, it is precisely this contrariness which gives it its precarious dynamics and hence its power. For let us not forget, it was those 'hillbilly cats' like Elvis and Jerry Lee who taught the world to rock 'n' roll.

la dolce vita

Offering a vision of what the future would look like

The geographic centrepoint of contemporary popular culture – *where it's at* – is constantly changing. In the 1940s, as we have seen, great pulsating bands of inspiration radiated out from Harlem to have their effect as far afield as Paris. In the early 1950s New York City's centrality was assured by the musical and visual innovations of bebop and the 'Cool School' of the Modernists. This influence continued to reverberate throughout the Western world well into the 1960s. But from around 1955 New York's monopoly on our cultural geography was challenged by a new and perhaps unexpected locale – Rome.

This continental shift marked the first time in which postwar popular culture was defined in European rather than American terms. Of course it isn't quite so simple. Presumably the Italians had taken note of the off-duty dress styles of the American GIs stationed in their midst during the war. Also, American jazz was extremely popular in Italy after the war and when Cool School trendsetters like Chet Baker performed there in the early 1950s, their minimal, casual apparel must have influenced the development of that style which would become known throughout the world as 'Italian'.

Cultural evolution in the modern world is rarely a respecter of national boundaries – modern communications and an international music industry having made us all (as McLuhan foresaw) part of one 'global village'.

Nevertheless, and despite the lines of influence which must be drawn back to the USA, Italy by the mid-1950s was rapidly becoming a place where the direction of popular culture is shaped rather than simply responded to. Though this culture did not

Epitomizing modern Italian menswear style, the always elegant Marcello Mastroianni in Federico Fellini's 1963 film, *8½*.

Casual, elegant, modern – mid-1950s *pavoneggiarsi* style. Illustration: Nicola Collings.

include innovative music, it did most certainly include design. From the Vespa to the Tubino light – Italian style in 1955 was already well on the way to becoming an international synonym of desirable.

Why Italy? This nation had long rejoiced in a network of craftsmen in all design-related areas who possessed the skill and the eye to fashion objects of excellence. And, fortunately, neither fascism nor the disruptions of defeat caused any long-lasting damage to this tradition.

Indeed, it was at least partly the very fact of Italy's defeat and the creation of a new, anti-fascist social order which propelled these craftsmen and designers towards a style which would loudly proclaim a complete break with the past. The resulting almost fanatical adherence to modernism was just what the rest of the Western world was waiting for. In 1955 – in North America, Britain or France – tomorrow had more cachet than yesterday.

When we focus on the issue of men's clothing styles, Italy had other factors working in its favour. Traditionally a country in which the working class as well as the upper class considered it not only a privilege but also a responsibility to dress well, Italy was well placed to provide inspiration for the working class of, for example, Britain, a country which was just beginning to discover a more democratic approach to style.

Secondly, Italy also offered to the world the role model of the *pavoneggiarsi* (peacock male) who struts and preens to his heart's content, oblivious of a more northern view which held that only women should concern themselves with cutting a *fare figura*. Italian men had never participated in the renunciation of masculine finery which had followed the French and Industrial Revolutions and now that men in Britain and North America were themselves reassessing this renunciation, the Italian male's swagger and sartorial flare provided justification as well as inspiration.

And, finally, the particular style of dress which evolved in postwar Italy was aesthetically appropriate to its historical moment. The sharp, short jackets and trim, tapered trousers which looked so right on a Vespa signified an easy, carefree, lighter approach to life. It was an approach which fitted perfectly within that notion of 'The Leisure Age' which was increasingly seen as the hallmark of postwar prosperity throughout the West.

All of which would be obvious by the time *La Dolce Vita* the film appeared in 1960. At least until toppled by London by the mid-sixties, Rome would serve as that shrine to modern living to which all jet-setting aficionados of the good life would make a pilgrimage.

But long before Fellini's cinematic vision captured it all on celluloid, Italian style had marched through Europe and crossed over to North America. The Vespa, the Gaggia espresso machine and the cleancut, modern lines of Italian menswear symbolized continental Europe's rise from the rubble of war and offered the Western world a vision of what the future would look like.

Live fast, love hard, die young. Ton-up Boys
(and one Ton-up Girl) gathering outside
London's Dorchester Hotel to take part in a
charity event.

A t the same time that *The Wild One*'s
prototypes were laying waste to
Hollister, California, British motorcyclists
were patiently waiting for petrol rationing to
end. Though this would happen in 1950, it
would take a few more years before any
subculture comparable to *The Wild One*'s
would emerge in Britain. And when it did, its
members would be known as 'Coffee-bar
Cowboys' or 'Ton-up Boys' rather than Bikers.

Coffee-bar Cowboys because they
tended to hang out in small, isolated roadside
cafés where they could drink coffee, show off
their bikes and challenge each other to
impromptu races. These cafés remained
obscure places, like Snitch's on the A10 or
Ted's on the North Circular Road, until the
Ace Café (also on the North Circular)
suddenly became so popular and notorious
that it got talked about in Parliament. Rows of
hundreds of gleaming bikes and the constant
coming and going of hordes of leather-
jacketed guys (and a few girls) made it clear
beyond doubt that Britain now had a fully
fledged Biker-style subculture.

Ton-up Boys – the term that caught the
media's attention – derived from 'doing the
ton', slang for the rite of passage of
exceeding 100 mph on your motorbike. As
both names suggest, the focus of this group
was racing and perfecting the performance
of your machine. In theory, therefore, Coffee-
bar Cowboys and Ton-up Boys were
sportsmen rather than a styletribe. In
practice, however, these young postwar
British motorcyclists were fine tuning a style
of dress which (while basically plain and
practical) would be profoundly influential right
up to the present day.

The Wild One was a key sartorial
inspiration. Although the film was banned in
Britain for some ten years after its US release
in 1954, posters and film stills showing
Brando *et al* in the Perfecto ('Bronx') style

coffee-bar cowboys & ton-up boys

leather jacket, jeans and boots were much prized. For most Ton-up Boys, actually acquiring such a jacket was difficult – at first because of limited availability, but later (when British firms like Lewis Leathers and Pride & Clarke began producing their own versions) simply because they were comparatively expensive garments. While some overcame this problem by resorting to the newly introduced hire-purchase schemes, others opted for the cheaper alternative of black vinyl. Whatever the jackets were made of, they were worn over a hand-knitted aran sweater, with jeans, and with a thick pair of white socks rolled over the top of chunky boots. Traditionally the look was embellished with a dazzling white silk scarf.

It all seems pretty innocuous now, but back in the mid-fifties, at a time when men of any age were expected to wear suits, it was a truly revolutionary look. The emphasis on leather, though today respectable and commonplace, was seen at the time as indicating an inclination towards criminality. As Johnny Stuart points out in his book *Rockers!*, the term 'leather-clad' had become a code word to signal delinquency and the media never missed an opportunity to use it to describe any suspect young person.[1]

Although there weren't many Ton-up *Girls*, a few did exist. In their uniform of leather jacket, jeans and boots, they demonstrated a unisex equality which would still cause shock and outrage in the 1960s. Herein lies an interesting contrast with the Teddy Boys and Girls, who also tended to come from the British working class. Both in their emphasis on visual differentiation between the sexes and in their eagerness to emulate an old-fashioned upper-class style, the Teds can be seen as inherently conservative.

The Ton-up Boys and Girls, on the other hand, though hardly revolutionaries in any

Two of the Ton-up Boys portrayed in the 1963 film *The Leather Boys*, which used the streets of London as an effective backdrop to this subculture's lifestyle.

accepted sense of the term, did present an image (never, in my view, a purely superficial phenomenon) which differed from the Ted's conservatism in that it found its inspiration in the future rather than in the past. (And owed nothing to the upper classes.)

At the Ace Café (used to good effect as a setting for the 1963 cult film *Leather Boys*) the rows of gleaming, streamlined bikes and the ubiquitous glint of black leather and PVC seemed to have come out of one of those 1950s futuristic science fiction films. And, beyond the image, both the unisex apparel of (however few) Ton-up Girls, and, for both

sexes, the 'Leisure Age' assumption that what you did in your spare time rather than what you did for a living defined your personal identity, suggest a break with the past. In this sense, the Ton-up Boys and Girls were arguably putting into practice that vision of a brave new world which the 1951 Festival of Britain had merely sketched out in abstract terms.

They were in fact very modern. So it is ironic that in the 1960s it would be their successors, the Rockers, who would form the opposition to those archetypal futurists – the Mods.

Left: Original 1950s West Coast Surfer style. Illustration: Nicola Collings.

Below: Transfer designed by Jasper Humphris, founder of Buz Clothing of Truro, Cornwall, makers of streetwear for Surfers.

but they too appreciated its offer of freedom. Certainly the Folkies' vision of the good life required a rural rather than an urban setting. And the Western-Style urban cowboy dreamed of life on the Great Plains, the Rocky Mountains or the deserts of the Southwest.

But while the cowboy myth hinged on the 'taming' of the Wild West, the Surfer wanted to live within and according to the rhythms of nature – to go with the flow. Both the Surfer's patience in waiting for just the right wave and his/her respect for the power of the sea is almost Taoist in character. Such attunement to and sympathy with nature has today become fashionable but in the 1950s it was out of step with an era which arrogantly assumed that science was destined to 'triumph' over nature.

The insights which the Surfers gained while riding the waves flavoured their entire way of life. Laid-back in the extreme, they chose a style of dress that was appropriately loose and casual. Energized by the intensity of their experience, they used bold stripes and slashes of colour in a way which set them apart from the drab Beats. Tanned skin, sun-bleached hair and bare feet or minimal sandals completed the original look – one which would remain fundamentally unchanged over many decades and which would influence millions of non-Surfers.

The transformation of surfing from sport to cult lifestyle took place in the early 1950s, but it was not until the late fifties and early sixties that the wider society began to look to the Surfers for inspiration. Here pop music played an important part: the Chantays, Jan & Dean and the Beach Boys provided the soundtrack. In the cinema, the *Gidget* films demonstrated how the carefree, hedonistic, Surfer lifestyle could fit neatly within the American Dream.

surfers

Like the Bikers and the Ton-up Boys, the Surfers took a sport and transformed it into a way of life. In one sense this was a very mainstream, 'Leisure Age' thing to do in the 1950s. But in another sense it was *dropping out*. Instead of confining recreational pursuits to your spare time, you said to hell with the nine-to-five life and set out for Malibu or the North Shore of Oahu.

This desire to 'get away from it all' is hardly unique to the Surfers. Bikers, Beats, Folkies and even Western-Style urban cowboys all wanted to turn their backs on the modern world. All sought a more authentic way of life, and all, at least in part, equated such authenticity with being in tune with nature. The Beats, even if just passing through the wide-open spaces of the USA or Mexico, felt its mystical rhythms. The Bikers may not have reacted so poetically to nature

Far left: Surf-Grunge look, worn at Newquay, Cornwall – Britain's foremost surf centre, 1993. Photo: Nicola Stanley.

Left: Local surf scene at Treyarnon Bay, Cornwall, 1993, with (*from left to right*): 'Soul Surfer', 'Grommit' (young hopeful) and competition surfer. The latter is sponsored by and wears clothes by *Sola*. Photo: Nicola Stanley.

Below: High fashion tries to 'hang ten' without getting its feet wet – Karl Lagerfeld for Chanel, Spring/Summer collection, 1991. Photo: Niall McInerney.

But if the Surfers' style and way of life seemed destined to dissipate into mainstream amusement, this would only be part of the story. Earlier, in discussing the Folkies, I suggested that they were the ancestors of the Hippies of the 1960s. This is true, but it is also true that some Hippies were in fact latter-day Surfers – pleasure-loving, carefree, casual and boldly colourful.

These are the sort of kids Tom Wolfe describes so vividly in his 1968 essay 'The Pump House Gang'.[1] Though hippyish influences are readily discernible, these teenagers in La Jolla, California, are first and foremost Surfers – waiting for the perfect wave, untroubled by that angst-ridden social consciousness which the Folkie-Hippies saw as central to their cause.

Which is not to say that the Surfers never rose above their fun-loving Beach Boy image.

Their early and insistent concern for the environment has always tempered their hedonism. Among many Surfers there exists a seriousness of purpose – almost a religion– which even in the 1950s was emerging as a model of how humankind might live in harmony with nature.

That Surfer subculture is still very much with us today and growing all the time. From Hawaii and the West Coast of America this way of life has spread to wherever there are waves to ride. And, in a very real sense, beyond that. For the fact of the matter is that today the bright, bold, casual style of the Surfers – and their easy, relaxed attitude – is ubiquitous. If LIFE IS A BEACH, rather than a bitch (as the Beats might have had it), it is thanks to that hardy clique of Surfers who back in the early 1950s sought a different kind of escape.

mods

While Jack Kerouac's *On the Road* summarized what had gone before in the history of streetstyle – the Zooties, the Hipsters, the Pachucos – Colin MacInnes's *Absolute Beginners* cast a prophetic eye on what was still to come. In particular, the ever increasing importance of what MacInnes's eighteen-year-old hero describes as 'this teenage thing'.

We have already seen the 'youthquake' rumbling on the Richter Scale, with the Rockabillies in the USA and the Teds in Britain showing an ever growing awareness of themselves as 'teenagers'. But by 1958, the year in which *Absolute Beginners* is set, this tendency was indeed (as MacInnes's hero says) 'getting out of hand'.

This is most evident in the way in which a new definition of the term 'generation' was emerging. By the late fifties, a generation gap could occur not only between parents and children but also between older and younger youths. Thus, in *Absolute Beginners*, 'Ed the Ted' (who would have been part of the youth revolution in the early fifties) has become one of the 'old style Teds' – not an absolute beginner – and therefore 'wasted'.

As we will see time and time again in the future history of streetstyle, each 'generation' seems compelled to define itself stylistically and ideologically as the opposite of the previous 'generation'. For the Absolute Beginners of 1958 this meant a rejection of the Teddy Boys' deliberately old-fashioned style and class-based identity. In its place came modern jazz, futuristic style and a determined attempt to define class as an irrelevance.

Left: Mods hanging out on Carnaby Street, London, 1964.

Right: The Zombies were not a Mod group but, like the Beatles and practically everyone else in mid-sixties Britain, they were clearly influenced by the Mods' sharp, less-is-more style.

Furthermore, while the typical Ted of the early 1950s may have readily embraced some aspects of American popular culture such as rock 'n' roll, he nevertheless retained a 'Little Englander' mentality which saw the English Channel as a fortuitous barrier against all things European. Not so the new generation of *Absolute Beginners*. Like the book's hero, they buzzed around town on Lambrettas, drank espresso, wore Italian-style suits, had their hair cut in the 'French' style and sat through 'New Wave' continental films. To be 'modern' was to be international and this new generation saw themselves as citizens of the world – embracing everything from Jamaican ska or black American rhythm and blues to Italian cuisine.

Within the broad spectrum of MacInnes's *Absolute Beginners* a key group were those who called themselves 'Modernists'. We have already seen how this styletribe emerged with the Cool School jazz musicians of New York in the early fifties as a reaction against the 'hot jazz' and gaudy style of the forties. We have also seen how by the mid-fifties the *pavoneggiarsi* of Italy extended this tendency into a total design aesthetic. But it was in Britain, at the end of the decade, that a small but fanatically dedicated band of Modernists transformed this style into a religion.

In *Absolute Beginners* the Modernists are most precisely represented by the character known as The Dean, who has

college-boy smooth cropped hair with burned-in parting, neat white Italian,

rounded-collar shirt, short Roman jacket very tailored (two little vents, three buttons) no-turn-up narrow trousers with 17-inch bottoms absolute maximum, pointed-toe shoes, and a white mac lying folded by his side.[1]
The Dean's female equivalent

sports short hemlines, seamless stockings, pointed-toed high-heeled stiletto shoes, crepe nylon rattling petticoat, short blazer jacket, hair done up into the elfin style. Face pale – corpse colour with a dash of mauve, plenty of mascara.[2]
International in outlook, deliberately blurring traditional gender boundaries, and decidedly street-smart, these kids are ready for a brave new world.

It is generally agreed that this new generation of British Modernists tended to come from lower-middle-class, often Jewish

backgrounds. However, it is unlikely that the individuals in question would have concerned themselves with such classifications – for them (unlike the Teddy Boys who explicitly saw themselves as working class), what mattered was not where you had come from but where you were going to.

But while class was being downgraded as an issue, *spending power* (as in North America) was increasingly important. Unlike, for example, the Beats, these *Absolute Beginners* celebrated the new Consumer Age. Most people did, of course – young and old – in the second half of the 1950s. But for the Modernists, a desire to demonstrate affluence was always secondary to a desire to demonstrate good taste – better to have one perfect suit than a dozen with the wrong number of buttons.

Above: **Archetypal Mod group the Small Faces, as they appeared on their first album in 1965.**

Top left: **Coventry Mods Mandy and Maria in tailormade hipsters in 1983. They describe themselves as 'cool, clean and hard'. Photo: Andy Clarke.**

Top centre: **Mod revivalist outside Kensington Market, London, 1980. Photo: Caroline Greville-Morris.**

Top right: **1980 ad from *Sounds* offering instant identification with Mod and Two-Tone revivals.**

By 1960 these dandies in the Beau Brummell tradition were regularly to be seen in certain coffee bars or jazz clubs in London admiring each other's tailor's handiwork. By 1962, as Nik Cohn says in his essay 'Today There Are No Gentlemen', 'there were enough converts to make a sect, which was called Mod'.[3]

But these were not the Mods that we visualize in retrospect. If they wore parkas, it was purely to protect their precious suits or expensive casuals from the rigours of a life lived on a Lambretta. Their almost puritanical aesthetic sensibilities would never have tolerated all the badges and scooter mirrors which epitomized the eventual stereotype. Like modern jazz, the original Mods lived by the creed 'Less Is More' and they would soon be sickened by the sacrilege being committed in their name.

Both the flowering of Mod as a subculture and its ultimate denigration as a style were set in motion in 1962 when *Town* magazine presented a feature on Mod style. The rest of the media soon followed suit and before the year was out 'Mod' had become the code word for all that was happening in an increasingly swinging London.

Despite this popularization of their style, the 'true Mods' held their own, at least for a while. Shops like John Stephen's His Clothes on London's Carnaby Street sold reasonably priced versions of the Italian, Cool School or 'city gent' styles. On the TV, *Ready, Steady, Go!* featured both authentic soul or rhythm and blues musicians like Rufus Thomas, Booker T and the MGs, Ray Charles, Otis Redding, Marvin Gaye, Martha and the Vandellas and The Supremes. In the audience, showing off their clothes and dance steps, there were always plenty of key Mod 'faces'. And what had begun as an almost exclusively male subculture now featured a strong female contingent which was perfecting a unisex style that would be hugely influential. It was indeed a Mod, Mod, Mod, Mod World.

But under the surface there were problems. The increasing popularity of purple hearts and other nerve-jangling

Left: **Clash of styles – the real thing versus the stereotype. Paul Weller with parka-clad fans in Oxford in 1984. Photo: Steve Pyke.**

Below: **'We're Mods . . . always will be . . . everyone else is just so *scruffy*,' London, 1980.**

amphetamines seemed at odds with that steady coolness of demeanour which had been central to the Modernists. At the same time, a new generation of even younger Mods seemed more interested in having a lark than in ensuring that their trouser seams were pressed to perfection. And many 'Mod' pop groups seemed to be just going through the motions in the interests of securing a larger following. (Years later Roger Daltrey of The Who would admit that he had really always been 'a Ted at heart'). The original inspiration of modernist purity seemed a world away.

In 1964 everything came to a head. As history and *Quadrophenia* will forever remind us, the Mods and the Ton-up Boys' successors, the Rockers, set upon each other in various seaside resorts. Though this provided good copy for the tabloid newspapers, media overkill would in time reduce both the Mods and the Rockers to caricatures of themselves.

At least in name, the Mods would live again and again and again in a never-ending series of revivals beginning in the late seventies and continuing into the present day. Although some of these tried to recreate the original Mod style and spirit as accurately as possible, others revived the caricature rather than the genuine article. Because the media, more often than not, focused on this latter group of revivalists, what had begun as sharp, immaculate, pristine and 'perfect' typically became its opposite: grubby parkas festooned with badges worn by kids who knew The Who's lyrics by heart but had never even heard of the MJQ.

And yet history should also record that around 1989, within the context of Acid Jazz, groups like the James Taylor Quartet rediscovered the Modernist tradition. Rather than simply pushing the replay button, these musicians and their followers set off in exciting new directions. While the standard issue Mod revivalist actually exhibited most un-Mod-like tendencies by dwelling in the past, these Acid Jazz Modernists were keeping alive that progressive spirit which had always been the true heartbeat of the Mod movement.

mods **53**

Bikes, leathers and rock 'n' roll: British Rockers in the early 1960s.

rockers

May 18, 1964, Brighton. A large group of Mods, brandishing deckchairs, force two lone Rockers to jump fifteen feet from the promenade to the beach below. The Mods are dressed in immaculate casual gear with wrap-around shades. The Rockers are in black leather jackets decorated with rows of metal studs and hand-painted insignia, their winklepickers as sharp as a flick knife. The image was splashed across the front of most British newspapers the following day.

Although such outright violence was not typical and although the events were greatly exaggerated by press, these were indeed significant moments in the history of streetstyle and youthculture. In particular, this was the first of what Peter York would years later call *Style Wars*. Unlike, for example, the 'zoot suit riots', which took place in the USA in the 1940s and which were at heart a racial conflict, the Mod/Rocker clashes of 1964 were motivated purely by differences in style.

In a sense, therefore, such events were supremely superficial. But this is to miss the point. In our age, style has become a language with the power to convey deeply rooted, complex attitudes and beliefs. At least within the context of streetstyle, appearance today always has an ideological dimension. The events which took place in Brighton and other British seaside resorts in the Summer of 1964 were no exception to this. Conflicting

These new Rockers rode out on a mission – to spread the gospel according to rock 'n' roll

styles were expressing alternative responses to changing social and cultural structures.

On one level this conflict was about class – what we would now categorize as 'blue collar' versus 'white collar' but which at that time was most potently expressed in the form of scruffy leather and jeans versus pristine casualwear and sharply pressed suits. But there is more to the story than this. The contrast between the Rockers' tough image and the Mods' softer look suggests changing definitions of masculinity. And perhaps too we can see in this stylistic clash different perspectives on the relationship of youth to mainstream society. The Mods, whose attire was essentially a refinement of respectable office dress, were plugged into the system – dressed for success. The Rockers, on the other hand, defiantly proclaimed their status as outsiders.

In the early 1960s the pace of history seemed to be accelerating and this was especially true within the arena of youthculture. As we have seen, the Mods did not acquire their name and begin to establish themselves as a unique subculture until 1962. The Rockers' history is even shorter: in 1962 those motorcycle enthusiasts who gathered at places like London's Ace Café were still known as Coffee-bar Cowboys, Ton-up Boys or Leather Boys.

Ironically, it seems to have been the Mods who coined the term 'Rockers'. But what they

Rocker Girl Judy Westacott at the 59 Club, Hackney, London, 1993.
Photo: Ted Polhemus and Sarah Tierney.

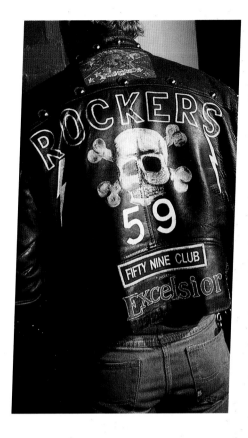

Opposite: Shaun and Rick, Rockers at the 59 Club, Hackney, London, 1993.
Photo: Ted Polhemus and Sarah Tierney.

Left: 59 Club badges and other Rocker insignia show how this subculture's style has evolved into the 1990s. The small figure hung on a chain is an EssoMan key ring – the same figure can be seen in the photo of early Rockers on page 54.

had intended as a put-down was received as a compliment by those younger Ton-up Kids who liked its association with foot-stomping rock 'n' roll. Throughout 1963 and into 1964, as the Mods grew in numbers and defined themselves more explicitly as a subculture, the Rockers did the same. The two groups forged their contrasting identities and styles in counterpoint.

Whereas the original Ton-up Boys' style had been plain and functional, the Rockers emphasized decoration – the painted insignia, rows of metal studs and heraldic badges creating a more overtly 'tribal' identity. And while the Ton-up Boys' subculture had been (at least ostensibly) tightly focused on motorcycles and 'burn-ups' (races), the Rockers' readily extended theirs to incorporate all facets of the rock 'n' roll lifestyle as defined by the likes of Eddie Cochran, Billy Fury, Gene Vincent, Vince Taylor and Johnny Kidd.

Instead of simply living to ride and race, these new Rockers rode out on a mission – to spread the gospel according to rock 'n' roll. And with good reason. Increasingly in the sixties the hard rocking tradition established by the likes of Elvis was being watered down, cleaned up and injected into mainstream consumerism in the form of 'Pop' (or, as the Rockers saw it, Pap). The Rockers took careful note of this and set about transforming motorcycle culture into the last bastion of rock 'n' roll authenticity.

The older Ton-up Boys didn't always see things this way. Noting that the more emphatic the sartorial decoration the less powerful the bike, they scoffed at this new breed of rebel. But, as the Mods' domination of British youthculture grew, the logic of the Rockers' stylistic extravagance was underlined. The original rock 'n' roll message did need to be reasserted in bold capital letters – the time for subtlety was long gone.

The Rockers' visual iconography of studs, painted insignia, chains and razor-sharp winklepickers was intended to leave no one in doubt that the spirit of hard-hitting rock 'n' roll was alive and kicking.

And so it came to pass that these 'gypsy outlaws'[1] journeyed to Brighton and other resorts in the Summer of '64 to stand up to the Mods. They were hugely outnumbered and by most accounts defeated. Indeed, for much of the sixties it seemed that the Rockers would become history. Today, however, we can see the folly of this presumption. Both on the street and on the fashion catwalk Rocker style is ubiquitous. Just as importantly, the Rockers' devil-may-care attitude and outsider's perspective inspired a 'rock culture' which stretches from the Headbangers to the Punks.

'The Godfather of Ska', Laurel Aitken, in his London home in 1979, wearing original Rude Boy style. Photo: Janette Beckman.

Jamaica gained its independence in 1962. It was around this time also that it began to devise a cultural identity which, while drawing heavily on African-American influences, 'cut 'n' mixed' these in a unique and special way. In the 1950s mobile sound systems had competed to bring to the dance halls of Kingston the latest, imported rhythm and blues records. But by the late fifties and early sixties DJs like Prince Buster were creating an indigenous music which was originally known as 'rudie blues'. Lingering on the off-beat and drawing on the distinctive rhythms of Rastafarian drumming, this uniquely Jamaican sound came to be known as bluebeat, rocksteady and, ultimately, ska.

Dress styles were changing as well. As in North America, Italy and Britain, the trimmed-down, sharp-as-a-razor *modern* look which had first surfaced with the Cool School jazz musicians of New York in the early fifties was making its presence felt in Jamaica. In particular, the notorious and much-feared streetcorner ruffians of Kingston who were known as Rude Boys began to exemplify this new style. In her important essay on black style, 'Rebel without a Pause', Carol Tulloch identifies the Rude Boy as 'Jamaica's first authentic subcultural street style'[1] and portrays him as 'dressed to rule the night in cropped, slim pants, bum-freezer leather or tonic jacket, intense shades and skiffle hair cut. The pork pie hat was an optional extra'.[2]

This Rude Boy look owed a great deal both to the Modernist American jazz musicians of the fifties and, in a more contemporary way, to the black soul musicians of the Tamla Motown tradition. But, as with ska, though such American influence is undeniable, the Rude Boy image must also be seen as distinctively Jamaican.

rude & boys two-tone

Multi-racial, multi-cultural
and, at the end of the day, often downright rude

As mentioned in the section on Caribbean Style in the 1940s, a tradition of backstreet, neighbourhood tailors throughout the West Indies had the effect of constantly producing new and unique styles. This seems to have been as true in the 1960s as it was in previous decades. Most immediately apparent in the case of the Jamaican Rude Boys was the short, 'cropped' trouser leg which ended above the ankle. (The story is told that when the Jamaican musician Desmond Dekker was brought to Britain by his record company and provided with a new suit, the first thing he did was to have six inches cut off the bottom of the trousers.) Also significant was the way in which the Jamaican Rude Boys tended towards shot fabrics like 'tonic' (or 'two-tone') which shimmer with contrasting colours. Midnight and electric blue were especially popular.

The total effect was one which succeeded perfectly in blending two seemingly irreconcilable aesthetic principles – the showy and the subtle. Whereas in the USA, in both progressive jazz and soul, the Modernist look had often tended towards a white, Ivy-League-influenced casual softness, in its Jamaican Rude Boy context it retained an aggressive, hard-edged quality which Dick Hebdige has described as 'almost abstract, almost metaphysical, intimating a stylish kind of stoicism – survival and something more'.[3]

This, of course, befitted the Rude Boys' life on the knife-edge in the difficult world of Downtown Kingston. Equally, this hard, sharp image suited the young West Indian in Britain who faced dire employment prospects, racial taunts and discrimination. At the same time, however, many young whites – Modish descendants of the *Absolute Beginners* – flocked to ska clubs and concerts and came

**London Rude Boy twins Chuka and Dubem Okonkwo, 1980.
Photo: Janette Beckman, *The Face*.**

to revere the West Indians' ultra-cool interpretation of modern style.

The effect upon British streetstyle was both profound and continuous. While the Mods were the first predominantly white subculture to pick up on Rude Boy styles, it was the Skinheads who – despite the subsequent racist inclinations of some of their followers – were most explicitly inspired by the Rude Boys' image and music.

In the late seventies the Rude Boy look was revived in a big way as 'Two-Tone'. Drawing in addition upon Mod and Skinhead styles (themselves, of course, partly influenced by the original Rudie look) and Punk energies, Two-Tone provided a refreshingly sharp contrast to the OTT excesses of the New Romantics of the same era. Two-Tone sold a lot of records, shifted a lot of tonic suits and, in the main, served to demonstrate an interracial harmony at a time when the rise of the National Front and other events made it difficult to be optimistic about the prospects for peaceful coexistence. From

the perspective of the original West Indian Rude Boys, however, it must have seemed as if many of the young white kids 'borrowing' their style and their music were cashing in on what they had created.

Nevertheless, the fact remains that such imitation had the effect of reviving interest in the original Rude Boy music and style and giving these an appreciative international audience. Two distant islands, linked by colonial exploitation and the historical circumstance of immigration, succeeded in making an impact worldwide which, arguably, neither of them could have managed on their own – for the first time bringing ska and Rudie style to the attention of mainstream audiences in Europe and the USA.

Both in the sixties and in the eighties Britain became, if only briefly, the centre of world popular culture. Invariably, it was *white* Britain which took the credit for this but the true source of such creative energy was multi-racial, multi-cultural and, at the end of the day, often downright Rude.

Above: **Half of Gaz Mayall – singer of The Trojans and DJ at London's longest running one-nighter club, Gaz's Rockin' Blues – wearing one of his original Rudie outfits from the 1960s.**

Right: **Two-Tone girls in Birmingham in the late 1970s, imitating the posture made famous by Madness and demonstrating the essentially unisex characteristics of this style. Photo: Janette Beckman.**

swinging london & the psychedelics

Above: The cacophony of style that was 'Swinging London'. Photo from *Carnaby St. W1*, a booklet produced in the late 1960s by the clothes shop I Was Lord Kitchener's Valet.

Above right: New Psychedelic Cindy Cat with an early 1980s interpretation of Swinging London artifice.

In 1964, when they were barely two years old, the Mods began to split into two opposing camps. On the one hand, there were the stripped-down 'Hard Mods' (much in evidence in the seaside clashes with the Rockers), who would gradually evolve into the Skinheads. On the other there was a huge number of what the media still termed 'Mods' but who in their ever more flamboyant, dazzling appearance were so in name only.

It is not surprising that the original Mod spirit of buttoned-down, minimalist restraint should have been swept overboard in the heady, exuberant atmosphere of 'Swinging London'. With the world's eyes fixed on British youth and with big money at stake in the pop and film industries, there was a constant temptation to emphasize the ostentatious at the expense of the refined.

Symptomatic of all this was what was happening down on Carnaby Street. A few years earlier it had been a fairly typical Soho backstreet, with newsagents, greasy spoon cafés and a few traditional tailors. In the early sixties it was transformed into a haven for the early Mods who discovered that menswear entrepreneurs like John Stephen had an eye for detail which matched their own. Then, as Swinging London became the centrepoint of the Western world's popular culture, an endless stream of new 'boutiques' opened on Carnaby Street, selling anything and everything that might catch the eye.

Vivid colour provided an obvious means of attracting attention – especially when unlikely, clashing shades were juxtaposed in the manner of Andy Warhol's recent paintings. Alternatively, inspiration came from

Op artist Bridget Riley and even from the Union Jack. To this cacophony of colour and pattern was added surplus decoration – most famously, rows of gleaming buttons and braiding reminiscent of traditional military and brass band uniforms.

All of which, jumbled together, produced an effect which was the precise opposite of the Modernist's 'Less is More' aesthetic. Nevertheless, the Swinging Londoners (and tourists) who flocked to Carnaby Street and the King's Road were faithful to one axiom of the 'True Mods' – that narcissistic dressing up was a male as well as a female option. Dress which had at first aroused mutterings of 'homosexual inclinations' when it entered the mainstream via pop music had become the unstoppable force known as the 'unisex revolution'.

But just as youth, pop, sex and capitalism were blending together into a potent concoction, the whole thing was losing its way stylistically. In the jumble sale which Carnaby Street had become it was hard to identify any theme or direction and harder still to find a name for that myriad collection of looks which Swinging London was now offering to the world.

By 1966, however, the word on the lips of the more 'with it' commentators was 'psychedelic'. Suddenly all those swirling Op/Pop designs, the clashing colours and the gaudy decorations made sense: Swinging London was just one big hallucination.

But though 'psychedelic' may have provided a useful label, it simultaneously marked the end of Britain's dominance of youthculture and shifted the focus, yet again, back to the USA. In the Summer of 1964, Ken Kesey and his band of 'Merry Pranksters' had taken an old school bus, loaded it full of tape recorders, movie cameras and the drug LSD

Above left: **Newburgh Street, which runs parallel to Carnaby Street, was the setting for this 1967 display of both Swinging London and Psychedelic styles.**

Top: **Far-out, 'Show Stopper!' outfit available through the *NME* small ads in 1970.**

Above: **Swinging London style from the shop I Was Lord Kitchener's Valet, in Carnaby Street.**

(at that time still legal in the USA) and set off on a journey criss-crossing the American continent in an attempt to 'stop the coming end of the world'. The bus was driven by none other than Neal Cassady (model for Dean Moriarty in *On the Road*) and painted inside and out in the most 'far out' array of colours in swirling patterns. So was born 'The Psychedelic Revolution'.

By the time the media caught up with all this, the Merry Pranksters would have become 'Hippies'. But as we shall see in the next chapter, the Psychedelic Revolution and the Hippies' 'Flower Power' were not one and the same thing. True, we can see the Pranksters' experiment as a source of both movements but, as the 'counterculture' evolved, their inherent stylistic and ideological incompatibility became more evident. The Hippy strand, in particular, would always be suspicious of the Psychedelic Revolution's love affair with technology and artifice. Just as importantly, despite history's labelling of all the descendants of the Pranksters as 'Hippies', the fact of the matter is that the Psychedelic Revolution was a force in its own right. (And one which would in time point directly towards the Ravers, the Technos and the Cyberpunks.)

More immediately, 'psychedelia' seems to be the description that best applies to what was going on in Swinging London in 1966 and 1967. Although the words 'Hippy' or 'Flower Power' might have been used, for example, to describe the 1967 'love-in' in London's Alexandra Palace, the predominant tone of what was taking place throughout London was too urbane, too sci-fi and too morally aloof to fit within this terminology.

This milieu is the subject of Michelangelo Antonioni's 1966 film, *Blow Up*. In it, a young, trendy fashion photographer happens by chance to take pictures of a murder. When he decides to 'do something about it', he is confronted by Swinging London's moral vacuum. Most relevant for our purposes is a key scene in a psychedelically styled nightclub where the audience comes alive only when the members of the band smash up their instruments in what is clearly an allusion to the destructive antics of The Who.

Like the club's décor, the styles of dress worn in this scene are within the territory of what might be called 'psychedelic': there are glittering, space-age fabrics which could have come from *The Avengers* and pastiche military uniforms reminiscent of the Beatles' *Sergeant Pepper* album cover. Was Antonioni exaggerating or had a point been reached in the history of Swinging London when exaggeration passed for reality? When one views documentary footage of scenes inside 'typical' Carnaby Street boutiques what one sees is, if anything, even *more* bizarre than Antonioni's fiction.

Call it 'Swinging London Style', call it 'Pop Style' or call it 'Early British Psychedelic', this was a time in the history of streetstyle when the outlandish passed as the mundane, when pop musicians looked more extraordinary than anything seen in *Barbarella* and when shops on Carnaby Street or the King's Road sold ordinary kids the sort of 'gear' that even today would cause disbelief.

All of which must have had the True Mods grinding their teeth in frustration. But in one important sense these flamboyant 'Psychedelic Mods' were just extending the brief set down by their original models. They were futuristic to the core and in this they were truly 'progressive' – tomorrow's Modernists kitted out for an intergalactic fancy dress party which Ziggy Stardust, Marc Bolan, George Clinton and Bootsy Collins would attend in due course.

Early 1980s New Psychedelics outside the Regal clothing shop, which served as a focus for this revival. Note that this is the same place – Newburgh Street – as shown opposite.

hippies

*A countercultural synthesis of
sorts did emerge – and the
reason for it was Vietnam*

Left: The Hippy Trail,
beginning or ending at the
statue of Eros in London's
Piccadilly Circus, 1971.

Below: By the early 1970s,
mass imports from around
the world allowed everyone
in the West – male and
female, young and old –
to identify with the
Third World.

Beats, Folkies, Surfers and Psychedelics – by the mid-sixties all the ingredients were assembled. The baby boomers' coming-of-age (with all its attendant media and marketing attention) turned up the temperature and before long the Hippy stew was bubbling away.

Since I have already described the direct predecessors of the Hippies, in a sense their story is already told. The Beats contributed a detachment from mainstream consumer society and a link back to the wellspring of Hipness itself: black jazz. The Folkies gave them a vision of simple, pre-industrial, rural life – and a belief in committed activism. The Surfers donated zestful hedonism and a direct, respectful link with nature. The Psychedelics brought mind-expansion and the possibility that modern technology (light shows, synthesized electronic sounds), new fabrics or colours, and LSD could be utilized to provide an escape route from the dreariness of modern life.

Of course when all these different elements came together on the West Coast of America in the period between 1965 and the 1967 'Summer of Love', what resulted was distinctive and greater than the sum of its parts. Or was it *less* than the sum of its parts? Did a fusion of all these elements ever really

Left: Here the ethnic influence comes from the West – in this case, native Americans – rather than from the East. Ad from *Disc* magazine, 1970.

Below: Hippies at the Rolling Stones' free concert in Hyde Park, London, 1969. Note again, as in the ads, the embroidered and fringed ethnic influences.

occur? To put it at its most provocative: Did the Hippies ever actually exist?

Certainly the label 'Hippy' (like 'Beatnik') was not warmly embraced (at least not in the early years). Originally, in the fifties, it had been a Hipster term of abuse – indicating someone who desperately wanted to be solidly in the groove, but clearly wasn't. It is unlikely that many of the sixties Hippies knew this, but what they did know was that the media gave the name 'Hippy' to everyone with long hair. In response, many would-be Hippies made a point of calling themselves 'Freaks' or 'Heads'.

But the problem was not only one of terminology. As a university student living in Philadelphia between 1965 and 1969, I (and everyone else with long hair) would regularly visit a string of 'alternative' shops on Samson Street, which was known as 'Big Street'. Some of these shops sold groovy psychedelic styles which seemed more inspired by Swinging London than by the 'love & peace' lifestyle centred on San Francisco. Alternatively, scattered among these were shops that sold garments which were hand-made from natural materials – often, as in the case of Afghan coats, ethnic in origin.

While all of this may have been broadly categorized as 'Hippy', the fact of the matter was that those who shopped in the futuristic psychedelic places were not generally interested in what was on offer in the 'back-to-nature' establishments – and vice versa. The same point could be made regarding music: there wasn't a great deal of cross-over between those into The Doors or Hendrix and those into Joan Baez or Dylan.

As someone who saw himself within the Beat strand of the alternative culture, I found *both* the Psychedelics and the back-to-nature/ethnic styles far too colourful to be hip. Likewise, I suspect that those long-haired California Surfers described by Tom Wolfe in 'The Pump House Gang' felt uncomfortable

Above: Hippy-style beads, patchwork flares, fringed shawl and floppy hat transferred to the catwalk for Dolce & Gabbana's Spring/Summer 1993 collection. Photo: Niall McInerney.

Right: The author in Mexican jumper, tie-dyed headband and patched denim flares (not shown), Oxford, 1972.

about being lumped together with many, if not all, of the other 'Hippies'.

In short, if the Hippies were a gathering of separate tribes they were not actually gathered very closely together. It could therefore be argued that those participating in 'The Summer of Love' were simply Beats, Folkies, Surfers and Psychedelics 'doing their *own* thing'.

Certainly in terms of both style and belief the differences could not be ignored. In the eyes of the Folk, Beat or Surfing Hippies, the Psychedelics' sci-fi futurism was often condemned as 'plastic' (which was just about the worst insult imaginable). Likewise, to those within the Folk camp, the Surfing or Psychedelically inclined were too blithely hedonistic to warrant genuine membership within the politically committed counter-culture. And to those of us in the Beat camp, everyone else seemed too hot and bothered – too 'sixties' – to be 'cool'.

Nevertheless, a countercultural synthesis of sorts *did* steadily emerge and the reason for it was Vietnam. As the body count mounted, as the news footage of the bombing raids grew ever more horrific, as the draft netted even middle-class white kids and as the war 'came home' in the form of the shootings at Kent State, differences within the counterculture became less significant. Concerted action was called for and this shifted the internal dynamics of the alternative culture towards those who had always embraced protest – the Folkies.

Thus did the term 'Hippy' begin to acquire a true identity. Nature triumphed over artifice. Committed, communal life pushed aside individualistic hedonism. Respect for ethnic lifestyles (from those of the native Americans to those of the Far East) overshadowed hip

urbanity. 'Flower Power' became a reality. (And I stopped wearing bohemian black, went colourful and bought myself an embroidered headband.)

When the war ended, once again the separate ingredients of 'the Hippy thing' reasserted themselves. The Surfers returned to their 'Endless Summer'. Psychedelic artifice would resurface in heavy metal, Glam Rock and Funk. The Beats went underground for a while but found new life in the jazz revival of the eighties.

And the Hippies? Many really did forge a counterculture and though for a time this seemed to be reduced to the pages of *The Whole Earth Catalogue*, their dream would once again find form among the Travellers and assorted 'Freaks' who decades later would strive to make the Age of Aquarius a reality.

British motorcycle gang, 'The Devil's Henchmen', stepping in to deliver the mail during a postal strike in 1971.

greasers

Ken Kesey's place, La Honda, California, 1965. The Merry Pranksters – just returned from touring the USA and the cosmos in their psychedelically painted bus – had a party. Their honoured guests were the Hells Angels. A good time was had by all.

While the Pranksters and their protégés the 'Heads' and the 'Freaks' would be the focus of the world media's attention within a year, in 1965 the spotlight was on the Angels. Almost two decades on from the incident in Hollister, California, which inspired *The Wild One*, this new generation of Bikers had become altogether different from their predecessors.

Their style was truly baroque. Chains, fringing and countless – often alarming – badges and insignia adorned their leather jackets (from which the sleeves had sometimes been crudely ripped off). Their image (and their reported exploits) made Brando's Johnny look tame.

A 1966 film called *The Wild Angels* (starring Peter Fonda) exploited the moral panic surrounding this subculture – and even featured some genuine Hells Angels (who later sued for defamation of character). When it was screened in Britain, this film aroused great interest. After all the publicity surrounding their clashes with the Mods in the Summer of '64, the Rockers had been cleaning up their image. Most famously, thousands of them had joined the 59 Club, founded by a motorcycle-riding vicar determined to prove that not all those who rode bikes were in league with the devil. Many Rockers felt that this PR exercise had gone too far, and when films like *The Wild Angels* and *The Cycle Savages* appeared, a sort of counter-movement set in which

Part of the contingent of Greasers at the Rolling Stones' free concert in Hyde Park, London, in the late summer of 1969.

their old-style rock 'n' roll authenticity, the Greasers used theirs to proclaim their badness. Though they were often called (or called themselves) 'Hells Angels', few were actually members of the official Hells Angels' chapters. But their demonic spirit and hellish image were clearly in the same tradition.

If, in 1964, the Rockers were operating in counterpoint to the smart sophistication of the Mods, by the late sixties, the Greasers were operating in counterpoint to the 'love & peace' initiative of the Hippies. And yet, just as Kesey's Pranksters and Sonny Barger's Hells Angels had found some common ground of anti-establishment rebellion, the release of *Easy Rider* in 1969 pointed towards a possible accommodation – however ideologically and stylistically strained – between Greasers and Hippies.

At the Rolling Stones' free concert in Hyde Park, London, in the late summer of 1969, a large contingent of Greasers were given free beer in exchange for providing security. Unlike at the Altamont Festival in California (where a fan was killed by a Hells Angel), there were no serious problems with this arrangement. But by this time, the daredevil motorcyclists and the Flower Children gathering to listen to the Stones had a third, opposing, force to contend with: the Skinheads. Compared to these alien creatures, even the Greasers and the Hippies felt as if they were on the same side.

sought to show that British bike boys (and a few girls) could look and act as demonic as these hell-bent Americans.

The Greasers, as they came to be known, wore jeans so soaked with oil that they positively glistened, and so frayed that two pairs were often worn as one. Their long, lank hair was partly covered by Second World War tin helmets or sinister peaked leather caps. Like their American models, they wore leather jackets that were often 'cut-downs' (sleeveless) or worn under cut-down, well-worn denim jackets. Ideally, every inch of leather or denim was festooned with chains,

studs, painted insignia or badges. And, while a 59 Club badge might be included in this decoration, the items that caught the eye were those Iron Crosses and swastikas which, though usually included only for their shock value, could not, for many, be divorced from their association with fascism.

Like the name 'Rockers', the term 'Greasers' was a put-down converted into a boast. If 'Cleanliness Is Next to Godliness', these 'Motorized Outlaws' (as Johnny Stuart called them[1]) wanted no one to be in doubt that they were on the side of the devil. While the Rockers had used their image to proclaim

Right: 'Beano', a London Skinhead, with a local policewoman in Petticoat Lane, 1980.

Below: Putting the boot in. The original Dr Martens' 11-eyelet model with optional steel cap. Available by mail order, 1981.

By the middle of the 1960s the Mods faced an awesome threat. Not the Rockers – you knew where you stood with them – but that glare of publicity and hype known as Swinging London. Suddenly *everyone* was a 'Mod'. But as these trendy imitators of Mod style proliferated, a small contingent of Mods decided to harden their image and get back to basics.

In the most immediate sense what this meant was a return to the sharp, stripped-down style of the original Mods. In music it meant a rejection of most of what was happening in the pop world and a rediscovery of the clean, no-nonsense rhythms of Jamaican ska, blue beat and rocksteady.

And with this rediscovery came the realization that the Rude Boys – highly visible in the small clubs that played this music – had created their own version of a genuinely modern style. The wrap-around shades, the trim two-tone suits, the white socks, the immaculately polished black shoes, the long black coats and the tightly cropped hair added up to a look which was precisely what Swinging London had turned its back on and forgotten.

The Rude Boys were *cool*. And, as first 'Psychedelia' and then the Hippies stepped into the limelight, coolness was an increasingly rare quality. Furthermore, the Rudies' style and attitude was *hard* at a time

skinheads

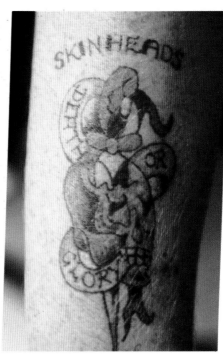

when everything from frilly Carnaby Street shirts to Hippy embroidered kaftans was soft in a deliberately feminine way. In short, despite differences of race and culture, the Hard Mods discovered that they had more in common with the Rude Boys than with the so-called Mods. As this realization grew, so too did respect and imitation.

But while racial divisions were being played down, class divisions were becoming critical. Unlike the original Mods, the Hard Mods came from classic working-class backgrounds and did not share their predecessors' view that class was an old-fashioned irrelevance. They observed that streetstyle and youthculture were being dominated (for the first time) by predominantly middle-class kids, in groups like the Psychedelics and the Hippies. Their response was to adopt an aggressively working-class identity: heavy boots and donkey jackets proudly proclaimed a life of manual labour. It was the incubation period for a new, distinctive British subculture – the Skinhead.

By 1968 they had arrived in their thousands – especially on the football terraces. By day they wore steel-toecapped boots, shortened and sometimes bleached jeans and buttoned-down Ben Sherman or collarless 'union' shirts; by night, Rudie-style mohair suits and well-polished brogues. The look was Modernist sharp, Rude Boy cool and working-class tough. (And, in its synthesis, uniquely British at a time when American influence was on the rise.)

Perhaps most importantly, here was a style which was the precise opposite of that of the Hippies. And what was true of appearance was also true of attitude and behaviour. Instead of 'love & peace', the Skinheads seemed to welcome conflict and (in many cases) physical aggression. At first this was focused primarily on the football terraces but soon there were instances of 'Hippy-bashing', 'queer-bashing' and 'Paki-bashing'. How typical such outright acts of violence were of the average Skinhead is hard to say. But looking as they did – so purpose-built for trouble – it was hard for the

British public to give the Skinheads the benefit of the doubt.

Ironically, perhaps just to keep everyone confused, many Skinheads at the turn of the decade smartened up their image. Wearing trim tonic suits and smart loafers, these 'Suedeheads', as their name suggests, also let their hair grow a bit – just long enough to pull a comb through. A few, in black 'Crombie' overcoats, bowler hats and carrying black umbrellas, almost resembled city gents. Finally, in 1971, hair got even longer and the name switched from Suedeheads to 'Smooths'. The Smooths *bore little resemblance to the early skins, although they were clearly of the same descent. This was the last phase in the development of the cult. It did not last long and had largely petered out by early 1972, when budgie gear, baggies and flares with turn-ups, glamrock and other new influences had taken over.*[1]

And that, or so it seemed, was the end of the story. However, when Punk surfaced in the UK in 1976 it had the effect of revitalizing

Left: Neville and Lee, Skinheads from High Wycombe, Buckinghamshire, 1985. Photo: Gavin Watson.

Centre: Kent, Japanese Skinhead, hanging out in Shibuya, Tokyo. Photo: Yurie Nagashima.

Below: Mandy Jarman has been wearing classic Skinhead styles for 14 years. Her suit was made by a local tailor to her own specifications using original 1970s two-tone fabric. The shirt is an original Jay Tex and the shoes are described by Mandy as 'old nursing shoes'. The photo was taken in Wolverhampton in 1991.

the dormant Skinheads. At the time, the Teddy Boys were undergoing a revival and when they clashed with the Punks it left the Skinheads wondering whose side they should be on. Some sided with the Teds but many younger Skinheads chose to align themselves with the Punks. It was all most confusing – especially as these two groups seemed to come from opposite ends of the style spectrum. Yet out of this bizarre confederation a new type of Skinhead emerged – combining shaved heads and/or colourful Punk mohicans with traditional items of Skinhead attire like chunky boots and braces. This subculture flourished under the name Oi!.

While the original Skinheads had retained respect for the West Indians who had given them a music to dance to and (in part) a visual style, a significant proportion of the Oi!s became linked with extreme right-wing political groups. Soon, thanks mainly to the media, Oi! (and by implication, the entire Skinhead subculture) became synonymous with racism. This view may not always have

been justified but once the association was made the course was set for racist, fascist Skinhead thugs to sweep throughout Europe, North America and Australia.

All of which, of course, is in direct contradiction to the Skinheads' original identity and roots. In the late eighties, first in the USA and then in Great Britain, a group calling itself SHARP (Skinheads Against Racial Prejudices) began making this point loud and clear. As their British founder Roddy Moreno says:

No true Skinheads are racist. Without the Jamaican culture Skinheads would not exist. It was their culture mixed with British working class culture that made Skinhead what it is.[2]

An alternative to the 'alternative'

funk

In the seventeenth century the word 'funk' meant fetid or stinky. In the twentieth century, among jazz musicians and other African-Americans, it was given a positive spin to accentuate that particular aroma associated with sex. More broadly, in the 1950s, 1960s and into the 1970s, its meaning among black Americans was one of erotic power and sexual desirability – denoting, ultimately, precisely that quality which uptight whites were seen to lack.

The adjective 'funky' was applied to everything – from black music to soul food. In terms of dress and adornment styles, the definitive expression of funkiness came in the early 1970s in the form of the Pimp Look, which surfaced in black ghettos across the USA – usually sported, as its name suggests, by pimps and other street hustlers whose comparative financial success allowed them (indeed, obliged them) to use their dress and their equally renowned 'pimpmobiles' as a way of advertising their affluence.

In this sense the Pimp Look fits squarely and logically within that Dressing Up tradition which we have previously identified with regard to the Zooties, the Pachucos and others from socio-economically underprivileged situations. The early 1970s 'funkification' of this approach simply accentuated the blatantly erotic, in-your-face sexual possibilities of dress. For example, enormous flares in the trouser legs served to focus the eye on the contrasting ultra-tight fit around the crotch and bottom (while the use of expensive materials like suede and snakeskin underlined the Dressing Up, aspirational aspect of the message.)

In his essay of the time, 'Funky Chic', the American writer Tom Wolfe includes an appropriately OTT description of the Pimp Look:

All young aces and dudes are out there lollygagging around the front of the Monterey Club [in New Haven, Connnecticut], wearing their two-tone patent Pyramids with the five-

inch heels that swell out at the bottom to match the Pierre Chareau Art Deco plaid bell-bottom baggies they have on with the three-inch-deep elephant cuffs tapering upward toward the 'spray-can fit' in the seat, as it is known, and the peg-top waistband with self-covered buttons and the beagle-collar pattern-on-pattern Walt Frazier shirt, all of it surmounted by the midi-length leather piece with the welted waist seam and the Prince Albert pockets and the black Pimpmobile hat with the four-inch turn-down brim and the six-inch pop-up crown with the golden chain-belt hatband . . . and all of them, every ace, every dude, out there just getting over in the baddest possible way, come to play and dressed to slay.'[1]

Wolfe's observations were exceptional. The white media in general still focused in the early 1970s on the mainly white, middle-class Hippies, and failed to take note of the sartorial magnificence of this important style.

The visual portrayal of the Pimp Look formed a key component of the 'Blaxploitation' films – most famously, *Shaft* in 1971 and *Superfly* in 1972 – which eventually succeeded in bringing an awareness of Funk outside the confines of the ghetto. But while the white counterculture yearned to embrace blackness in general and sexual funkiness in particular, it found the Pimp Look featured in these films hard to accept. The Hippies disliked its celebration of artifice and for all sections within the counterculture its aspirational tendencies jarred with their anti-materialistic inclinations.

Nevertheless, Funk's appeal was hard to resist and just as the Hipster had crossed the racial divide from black to white, the white counterculture (and its trendy entourage) came to embrace 'Funky Chic'. But as Tom Wolfe points out, in this instance the cross-over was largely terminological, with Dressing Down, middle-class whites typically retaining that casual, scruffy style which had become the uniform of the counterculture. More *Woodstock* than *Superfly*, frayed denim rather than snakeskin, VW Beetle rather than 'pimpmobile', the 'Funky Chic' which became all the rage among whites in New York, LA and San Francisco missed the point because those who adopted it 'never bothered to look at what the [black] brothers on the street were actually wearing.'[2]

Arguably, this was less true across the Atlantic in Britain, where, fusing with existing Psychedelic styles, the energetic innovations of Funk may well have been important in providing inspiration for the Glam looks which we will consider in the following chapter. And perhaps, too, the intergalactic apparitions of Ziggy Stardust *et al* eventually inspired the American black Funksters to accentuate the cosmic over the aspirational. At any rate, by the mid-1970s, the likes of George Clinton and Bootsy Collins were descending on the Rock establishment like funky aliens from a distant galaxy.

Above: The definitive Funkster, George Clinton, in 1979. Photo: Janette Beckman.

Left: Looking cosmically funky as always – Bootsy Collins performing at the Ritz in New York City in 1993. Photo: David Corio.

glam

Left: Space oddity David Bowie posing for the cover of his single 'Sorrow', which was released in 1973 during his *Hunky Dory* period.

We take Glam for granted (or we take it as a joke) but how different things would be without it.

For decades streetstyle had been battling against the belief that Western man should forego finery, make-up, exotic hairstyles and any delight in his appearance. Almost every styletribe we have considered – from the Zooties to the Greasers – has stoically chipped away at this bizarre restriction. The Mods, Swinging London, the Psychedelics and the Hippies succeeded in putting the concept of 'unisex' on the agenda, yet none of them quite broke through the barrier.

When in the late sixties 'political', 'serious' issues and 'anti-fashion' took centre stage, 'unisex' more often than not came to mean simply that *both* sexes would abstain

Bowie lookalikes, waiting to get into his concert at Earls Court, London, in 1973.

from frivolous finery. Especially in the USA, but also in Britain, the transition from the sixties to the seventies saw a time in which streetstyle and youthculture were increasingly dominated by Leftover Hippies whose idea of style was to look as if you never took a bath and were so caught up with matters of cosmic importance that you just threw on a pair of battered jeans and a T-shirt.

What Glam did was to insist that such apparently superficial and frivolous matters be recognized as part of the revolution. Marc Bolan and David Bowie were key players in this process. Both had been through a great many changes, adroitly shifting from Mod to Psychedelic to Flower Power at the appropriate moment. However, at the point when they metamorphosed into, respectively, the Cosmic Crusader and Ziggy Stardust/Aladdin Sane, they began to make history rather than simply accommodating themselves to it – by making unisex a reality rather than a theory.

Decades on we can appreciate that stylistically there were important similarities between the Glam look which Bowie, Bolan and others created in Britain and the Cosmic Funk look which was developing in black America. What the two styles most obviously shared was a distaste for the scruffy anti-style of the un-evolving Hippies. Both reacted to the 'back-to-nature' ethos/aesthetic by going interplanetary to explore the possibilities of artifice.

Where Glam and Funk differed from each other was in their earthly context. The socio-economic realities of the black urban ghettos of the USA obliged Funk to focus on ostentation as a demonstration of personal success. Glam's roots, on the other hand, were in a Swinging London whose comparative prosperity meant that stylistic

experimentation was free to serve simply as an expression of personal identity. In particular, this expression took the form of experimentation with gender roles. Both in their appearance and in their forthright espousal of bisexuality, Glam musicians like Bowie and Bolan challenged our culture's traditionally highly restrictive, inhibiting definition of 'masculinity'. The extent of their success in this challenge is Glam's most significant achievement.

All of which George Clinton and Bootsy Collins would address in a very funky way before the decade was out. But 'androgyny', as it was called, was central to the Glam experiment from the beginning. From the moment that Bolan and Bowie put on vibrant make-up and dyed their hair in shades of Crazy Colour, the course was set for a radical rethink of masculinity. The Punks, the New Romantics and the Goths were their immediate heirs.

For no matter how extraordinarily bizarre Glam musicians may have looked on stage, they were slavishly imitated by their fans. And not only at concerts. Before 1972 was out hordes of adolescent Ziggy Stardust

lookalikes could be seen in city centres throughout Britain. With matching hair, glittering, space-age outfits and chunky platform shoes they were like an alien army from Mars which had suddenly come to planet Earth. Comedians made jokes about them and cartoonists caricatured them but this only served to underline the sense of unease that they provoked.

And for good reason. Suddenly it was clear just how little Swinging London and all that had actually deviated from the norm. Suddenly the Mods and the Rockers, even the Psychedelics and the Hippies, looked like ordinary kids having a good time. These Bowie clones, on the other hand, were *alien creatures* – space oddities – who seemed to have no links with British or, for that matter, earthly life.

At the heart of this deviance (and the real trigger of all the anxiety) was the fact that these kids did not seem to relate at all to traditional definitions of gender. Though 'You can't tell the boys from the girls' had been said of the Rockers, Mods and Hippies, now it was almost literally true. From here on, anything was possible – indeed, likely.

rastafarians

The Rastafarian movement started in Jamaica in the 1930s, after Haile Selassie (Ras Tafari Makonnen) was crowned emperor of Ethiopia. Interpreting this coronation as the fulfilment of a biblical prophesy, the early Rastafarians took heart in the dream of a black 'Zion' which would eclipse the white-dominated 'Babylon' which surrounded them. Accordingly, thousands of mostly poor Jamaicans (both in the slums of Kingston and scattered throughout the hills) awaited the day when they might return to their African homeland.

Until that day came, Rastafarians sought to distance and insulate themselves from 'Babylon's' soul-destroying ways. They looked for inspiration to the ancient civilizations of Africa – in particular to Ethiopia, which linked this past with the present. At the same time, they adopted a way of life which emphasized peaceful tolerance, personal dignity and the rediscovery of those natural harmonies which the modern world, in its greed, industrialization and artifice, had long forgotten. These beliefs would shape the development of Rastafarian style.

By the early 1970s a substantial number of West Indians were demonstrating their Rastafarian beliefs by wearing belts, hats, 'tams' (knitted caps), epaulettes, badges, scarves, wristbands and T-shirts made in the sacred colours of the Ethiopian flag – red, gold and green. From the Rastafarian's desire to live in harmony with nature came an emphasis on garments made from natural fabrics and, also, a distinctive hairstyle – dreadlocks – which required no artificial

products for its creation or maintenance. The international success of Bob Marley and other Jamaican reggae musicians served to make both the colours and the long 'locks' synonymous with Rastafarian beliefs.

Jamaica's Rastafarian population was swollen in the early 1970s by the addition of a high proportion of Kingston's Rude Boys, who aligned themselves with the Rastafarian cause, giving up their two-tone suits in shimmering electric and midnight blues in favour of the looser, more casual Rastafarian style. In Britain, as in Jamaica, the dreadlocked Rastafarian in a huge 'tam' and often wearing army surplus clothing (in sympathy with Rastafarian Cuban 'Freedom Fighters' in Angola) became a common sight. Rastafarian women also made their presence felt by dressing in long, African print skirts and sandals, dispensing with make-up and wrapping their dreadlocks in traditional African headdresses.

As 'Rasta Style' grew in popularity, a split developed between 'true Rastafarians', for whom appearance was only an outward

Above left: 'Natty Cultural Dread', from Big Youth's 1976 album for Trojan Records.

Above: Rastafarians in Notting Hill, London, mid-1980s.

expression of deeply held beliefs, and 'false Rastas', who liked the look but had only a superficial involvement in terms of beliefs and values.

But this tendency on the part of some young blacks to treat Rastafarianism as 'just a fashion' was nothing compared to what would happen in the 1980s when many of London's trendy white kids (including Boy George) began to sport (usually) artificial dreadlocks. On Boy George's part this may have been a genuine attempt to advance the ideal of the world as a 'Culture Club' embracing all races and beliefs, but its effect was to take a style which had originally served as a visual expression of religious belief and remove from it all meaning except 'I'm trendy'. In Babylon, the true is made false, the symbolic is made arbitrary and the authentic is made into fashion.

Above left: Bunny Wailer – one of the original Wailers – in military camouflage and African-inspired dress, London, 1990. Photo: David Corio.

Above: Religious symbolism reduced to fashion – from Rifat Ozbek's Spring/Summer 1991 collection. Photo: Niall McInerney.

headbangers

In the late 1960s, youthculture was increasingly dominated by the 'counter-culture'. In effect this meant a shift towards the middle class, the university educated and, especially in rock music, towards artsy sophistication. All of which was a long way from the straightforward gutsiness of the original rock 'n' roll which had been a product of the ghetto and the working class. This imbalance had to be redressed and when in 1968 the pop group Steppenwolf included the phrase 'heavy metal thunder' (from William Burroughs' *The Naked Lunch*) in their hit 'Born To Be Wild', the term seemed to suggest a music and a lifestyle which, though progressive, would be more mindful of its rock 'n' roll roots.

Both musically and stylistically, 'heavy metal' rapidly achieved 'an unexpected marriage of hippy and rocker culture'.[1] It drew inspiration from both Psychedelia (Hendrix, The Doors) and Flower Power (look at early Led Zeppelin), but it quite literally took an

'axe' to the tendency of both movements towards the pretentious and the precious. Here was a return to no-nonsense rock 'n' roll fundamentals and things like simply having a good time (which had been pushed aside by the counterculture's preoccupation with political activism).

In terms of dress style, heavy metal managed a remarkable fusion between earthy, Hippy-style scruffiness (battered denim, long hair), Psychedelic (and, later, Glam) glitz and Rocker-style studded leather. While individual groups tended to emphasize one particular style influence over the others, the subculture as a whole was so cohesive that it succeeded easily in embracing them all (precisely what the counterculture had failed to achieve). All that heavy metal needed was a tribal name which could describe the group as well as its music. Someone, somewhere, came up with the term 'Headbangers'.

As the Headbangers grew in numbers and further defined themselves as a subculture

Above: Classic Headbanger style available by mail order through the music press, mid-1970s.

Below: The influence of Hippy style is evident in this 1970 photo of heavy metal band Black Sabbath which appears inside their album *Paranoid*.

Heavy metal embraces two distinct stylistic traditions. The scruffy denim look, which derives from the Hippies, is shown *opposite* and on pages 82 and 83. Shown here are two examples of the sexy leather look, deriving from Glam. Both photos were taken by the author in 1993 in London's Kensington Market. *Left*: 'English Warlords'; *below*: 'Red Balls of Fire'.

The Headbangers have demonstrated that styletribes can exist outside of time, oblivious to passing trends

Above and right: Back and front views of a heavy metal fan at the 'Monsters of Rock' festival, Castle Donington, Wiltshire, 1992. Asked how long he had been collecting badges, he replied, 'Only since 1974'.

DIY jacket art found at the 'Monsters of Rock' festival, 1992. The variety of subject matter and style underlines the heterogeneity which exists today within the heavy metal scene.

they increasingly became the butt of ridicule and the target of outright criticism. In the late 1970s a peak of abuse was reached which is perhaps without equal in the entire history of streetstyle. This hostility came not only from the older generation but also from the Headbangers' own contemporaries. Young, 'alternative' music critics dismissed the heavy metalists as crude and retrogressive. The Hippies saw them as uncouth and unenlightened. To the tabloid cartoonists they were the ultimate youthculture joke – the lank-haired, gangling youth pounding an imaginary 'air guitar' with his earhole pressed tight against an enormous, thumping speaker.

And such stereotypical Headbangers did exist. But at the same time it should be recognized that underlying such caricature was a significant element of snobbery. Whereas the media is all too typically urbane and middle-class in outlook, heavy metal's appeal is most strikingly felt in the backwater provinces and among the working class.

Though heavy metal extremists have sometimes been rightly criticized for misogynist diatribes and irresponsible allusions to Satanism, it might be argued that the core of the critical abuse directed at this subculture over the years has derived from an anti-provincial and anti-working class prejudice.

In 1993 I attended the famous 'Monsters of Rock' festival at Castle Donington in Wiltshire. I went, with my camera, and with great trepidation – assuming at best that I would stick out like a sore thumb (which I did) and at worst that these ferocious heavy-metal fanatics would react aggressively to my presence. What I found instead was a huge throng of good-natured kids who were happy to pose for my camera and genuinely pleased to answer my questions.

I say 'kids', but the fact of the matter is that at the 'Monsters of Rock' festival – among fans and musicians alike – a wide range of ages were represented. This too is significant. Dozens of different styletribes have emerged since the early seventies but

many have been belligerently ageist and few have grown old gracefully. The Headbangers, on the other hand, have demonstrated that styletribes – like the 'real' tribes of the Amazon or New Guinea – can exist outside of time, oblivious to passing trends.

This is not to say, however, that heavy metal is simply standing still. An extraordinary collection of musical sub-styles have gathered under its umbrella: satanic/black metal (e.g., Black Sabbath, W.A.S.P.), glam metal/sleaze (e.g., Motley Crue, Hanoi Rocks), thrash metal (e.g., Metallica, Sepultura) and death metal (e.g., Slayer, Paradise Lost), all attracting their own devoted followers. At the same time, different styles of dress have emerged which are appropriate to each musical specialization. Perhaps most importantly, the 'poodle' haircuts, Spandex jeans, leather, snakeskin, leopard prints and profusion of metal accessories associated with glam rock and sleaze metal have provided a much needed antidote to the at times almost ubiquitous badged-denim look.

northern soul

Throughout much of the 1960s, American Soul musicians found a warm welcome and a home away from home in Britain. But when the Mod scene fractured into the Psychedelics on one hand and, on the other, the Hard Mods (precursors to the Skinheads), interest focused on progressive rock and Jamaican ska. In Britain, as in the USA, soul suddenly seemed less important and less relevant.

At any rate, that was how it looked through the eyes of the London-based media. Up North, in places like Droitwich, Wolverhampton, Stoke, Nottingham, Manchester, Liverpool and Leeds, a new generation of kids were determined to keep the Mods' beloved soul music alive.

'Northern Soul' (as it was dubbed by *Blues & Soul* journalist Dave Godin in 1970) focused on a dedicated, even fanatical network of DJs and amateur enthusiasts who bought up and hoarded obscure, often pre-Motown singles and devised ever more complicated, highly acrobatic dance steps. They congregated in places like the Torch in Tunstall, the Mecca Ballroom in Blackpool, Va-Va in Bolton, the Twisted Wheel in Manchester, Samantha's in Sheffield and, most famously, the Casino in Wigan. Many of these venues put on 'all-nighters' and it became a way of life for 'Soulies' from all over Britain to make weekend-long pilgrimages to these events.

Music and dancing were always the key to Northern Soul, but a distinctive style of dress soon emerged. Naturally this style had to be suited to strenuous dancing, so loose, comfortable clothes were an obvious choice.

This was most strikingly seen in trousers known as 'baggies'. These flared from the waist rather than the knee and ended high in the ankle (the better to show off your white socks and fancy footwork) at anything from twenty-four to an awesome fifty inches wide. The waistband was also wide (up to eight inches) and kept in place by plastic-toothed waistband adjusters rather than a belt. Personalized detailing was all-important, and since no garment bought off the peg could survive careful scrutiny, the done thing was to have a tailor make one up to your own specifications, in chocolate brown, Prince-of-Wales check, blue denim or black needlecord. (The equivalent garment for girls was a long, mid-calf, circular skirt which would flare out when you were dancing.)

By the mid-seventies the Northern Soul scene was massive. Yet, intriguingly, it remained largely invisible to the outside world. The media was still preoccupied with the Leftover Hippies and the music industry (rightly) saw no profit in records whose value derived precisely from their rarity. While those other post-Mods, the Skinheads, would become notorious throughout the world, the Northern Soulies remained a carefully kept British secret – unknown even to many in the UK. Their peak years were from early 1974 to 1976 but they revived in the 1980s.

Stylistically, they seem to have made little impact. Perhaps they gave the Bay City Rollers their baggy trousers and perhaps they played a part in popularizing the 'wedge' haircut which would become ubiquitous in the late 1970s and early 1980s. But their influence ends there. One is tempted, therefore, to

dismiss the Soulies as an interesting but irrelevant footnote in the history of British youthculture. But this is to miss one important point. The kids doing their backflips and high kicks at the Wigan Casino were young – Absolute Beginners – and as such they represented a new, post-Hippy generation. Northern Soul was where this generation first discovered that they too could create an underground subculture. They would go on to become the Punks, the New Romantics, the instigators of 'club culture' and the driving force of international streetstyle for many years to come.

Above: **Northern Soul dance steps observed at the Wigan Casino by artist and enthusiast Mark Wigan, who went so far as to name himself after this definitive Northern Soul venue. He also drew the Northern Soul Boy** *opposite*, **showing the typical dress style of 1978.**

Below: **Northern Soul style by mail order, including (*bottom*) 34-inch 'bags', available from Bogeys in a range of styles – pleated, zipped, buttoned, flapped or patched.**

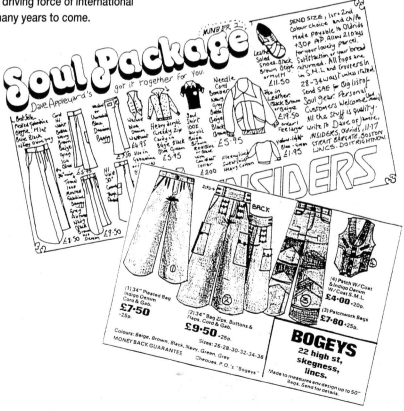

skaters

egend has it that some kid who wanted to be a Surfer but lacked the necessary transport to get to the beach took the wheels from a pair of rollerskates and fixed them to a plank of wood, so becoming, in the words of the Jan & Dean song, the first 'Sidewalk Surfer'.

Skateboarding became an enormous international craze early in the 1970s. But despite (or, more likely, because of) its popularity, Skaters did not begin to form into a coherent, visually identifiable subculture until much later in the decade. Up to this point skating was something which practically all adolescent boys took up at one time or another – a hobby rather than an identity, a sport rather than a way of life.

Skaters probably became a 'tribe' in their own right because Joe and Jane Public, tired of dodging supersonic teenagers on the way to the supermarket, succeeded in having skateboarding banned from most popular public places. Banished to remote, often desolate locations where they made use of discarded bits of concrete or created self-made ramps, Skaters became outsiders. And when they did indulge their obsession in public places, they were harangued, moved on or fined by the police – experiences which fostered an 'attitude' that further contributed to a sense of group identity.

As far as appearance style was concerned, however, there was little to distinguish Skaters from Surfers. Both groups wore extra-large, brightly patterned 'baggies' (long, oversized shorts), bold, graphic T-shirts and 'Vans' (a particular brand of American sneakers/trainers). This style had been invented by the Surfers and it was logical that their sidewalk counterparts should find it appropriate to their needs. In addition, the

Right: A Japanese Skater in Osaka, with customized board and trainers, 1992. Photo: Norbert Schoerner.

Below: An American Skater in London in the late 1970s demonstrating 'rock 'n' roll' manoeuvre and original Surf-Skate style crossover.

Bottom right: The bright, bold Skater style which was popular in Britain in the late 1980s.

despised rollerskaters typically wore tight-fitting, Lycra 'disco' styles and the Surfers' voluminous 'baggies' were a sure way of proclaiming the Skateboarders' separateness from this group. The Surfers already patronized established companies such as OP (Ocean Pacific), Offshore or Quicksilver, which sold their favourite streetstyles, and the Skaters simply began to buy from the same outlets.

In the late seventies, however, the rise of Punk had the effect of driving a wedge between many Skaters and their Surfer comrades. Scanning the blue horizon while waiting philosophically for the perfect wave, the Surfers had an empathy with nature which made them unlikely candidates for Punks' celebration of artifice and urban decay. The Skaters, on the other hand, already inhabited a world of concrete and – frequently at odds with the authorities – already possessed the makings of Punk-like alienation and rebellion.

Such ideological common ground promoted stylistic imitation. This is not to say, however, that these American Skaterpunks came to resemble Johnny Rotten or Siouxsie Sioux on wheels. But then neither did the vast majority of *non*-skating Punks in North America, whose style usually omitted the more extreme visual elements of their British counterparts. Instead of fishnets, facial piercings, rubber/PVC fetish garments and towering mohicans, all but a tiny minority of North American Punks contented themselves with an eclectic mix of 'thrift shop' bargains, oversized lumberjack shirts, a high proportion of black garments and cropped, obviously bleached hair – all put together to give an air of studied scruffiness. It was this look which became the uniform of most of the American Skaterpunks (and which, incidentally, paved the way for that other important punkish American style, Grunge).

Skaterpunks (or, perhaps, Punk Skaters) are still to be found in the USA but in the mid-1980s a new generation of Skaters began to emerge both there and in Britain. Arguably reflecting the success-oriented ethos of the Reagan/Thatcher era, this new group were far removed from the Skaterpunks in both style and attitude. Instead of cheap, second-hand attire, they preferred 'box fresh' garments with prominently displayed, upmarket logos.

The problem, however, was that (increasingly in the late 1980s) these same styles and logos (e.g., Pervert, Jive, Fuct and, in Britain, Insane, Poizone and Bench Clothing) were becoming popular with trendy types who had never risked life and limb on a skateboard. For the Skaters, the only obvious solution to the problem of imitation by undesirable outside elements is continually to change their style in order to retain their authenticity. Needless to say, this is an expensive business, but it has had the positive effect of keeping this subculture dynamic, creative and stylistically innovative.

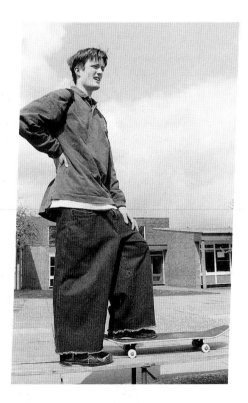

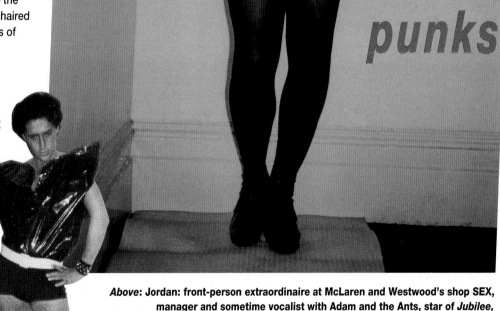

I n January 1976 the *New Musical Express* ran an article headed 'During The Course Of This Year All The People Pictured Here Will Be 30 Or Older'. The people referred to included practically every major rock musician of the time. What had begun some ten years previously as a 'youth revolution' had become a gerontocracy of 'boring old farts'.

It was time for a *new* 'youth revolution' and clearly it would have to define itself in opposition to the 'baby boom' generation's Leftover Hippies. Instead of back-to-nature and 'flower power': acidic artifice. Instead of love & peace: aggressive toughness. Instead of the slick 'megagroups' which increasingly dominated rock music: a rough-and-ready, learn-three-chords, brash amateurishness. Instead of kaftans: black leather jackets. Instead of the Age of Aquarius: 'No Future'.

Punk was the only obvious retort to the smug faces of all those thirty-plus, longhaired popstars exhibited in the *NME* like relics of another era.

punks

Above: Jordan: front-person extraordinaire at McLaren and Westwood's shop SEX, manager and sometime vocalist with Adam and the Ants, star of *Jubilee*, and key figure in the initial rise of Punk. At home, 1977. Photo: Caroline Greville-Morris.

Left: Another original and highly influential Proto-Punk, Philip Sallon, shown here with friend Yelena in 1976. 'We just got this idea to make outfits out of bin liners. It was the first time anyone did it. For a while it looked unique, but then everyone started copying it.'

The Punk approach to DIY leather jacket art, as seen on the King's Road in the early 1980s (*above*) and the late 1980s (*top*). In all cases the name and logo of a favourite band has been elaborated to make it an intrinsic part of a customized, unique appearance.

Early in 1976, however, Punk didn't even have the legitimacy (or the straightjacket) of a name. There was just an odd assortment of kids from London and its suburbs who spent a lot of time together commiserating about how boring everything was. (And it was!) Sociologically, these Proto-Punks had little in common. They were not, as is often assumed, all working-class slum-dwellers. A few were, but most were middle-class, even suburban. What they shared was a hatred of the remains of the counterculture (*sic*) and a determination to push them aside.

On Saturdays they migrated in mass to London and in particular to the 'wrong' end of the King's Road. Appropriately called 'World's End', this section had never enjoyed the trendy prosperity of the rest of this famous street. Both in name and in ambiance, it was a suitably down-at-heel location for the launching of the Proto-Punk revolution.

And this wasn't all that World's End had to offer. Since 1971, two larger-than-life characters named Malcolm McLaren and Vivienne Westwood had been running a small clothing shop at 430 King's Road. As 'Let It Rock', it catered for Teddy Boys and Rockers. In 1974 it was transformed into 'Too Fast To Live, Too Young To Die' and offered fetish garments of the sort previously available only by mail order in discreet brown paper parcels. In 1975, carrying this theme to its logical conclusion, it became 'SEX' – its name displayed on the front of the shop in ten-foot-high fluorescent pink plastic letters.

SEX's kinky shop sign was not only an affront to the normal standards of good taste but also an assault on the back-to-nature aesthetic and lovey-dovey principles of the Leftover Hippies. The Proto-Punks lost no time in adopting it as their meeting place and SEX quickly became a focus for a new, truly alternative subculture. Not content with this, McLaren decided to put together a rock band. The Sex Pistols (named after the shop) were intended (at least in part) to serve as

models for Westwood's latest creations and thereby attract attention to the shop. History records that they would accomplish this in a way and to an extent which probably exceeded even McLaren's expectations.

It is undeniable that the combination of the Sex Pistols, McLaren's irrepressible spirit and Westwood's innovative designs was instrumental in shaping Punk and in promoting it beyond World's End. But it is also certain, in my view, that even without them something big and bold, energetic and outrageously shocking would have happened. One has only to look at the extent to which parallel (even precursive) developments were taking place in the USA. In particular, New York's CBGB club scene and the un-Hippy-like characteristics of American musicians like Richard Hell, Patti Smith, Television and the New York Dolls suggests an evolution of Punk which begins with Lou Reed and Iggy Pop and which only reaches Britain after its essential, mutant qualities have been well established. (Let us note that Malcolm McLaren briefly managed the New York Dolls in 1975 and returned to London with Johnny Thunders' guitar which he symbolically presented to the Sex Pistols.[1])

Extraordinarily powerful seismic forces were poised ready to rupture the seemingly stable surface of the mid-seventies and had McLaren and Westwood not been around to toss a few sticks of dynamite in the right direction an eruption would have occurred anyway. And it would, I believe, have inevitably taken roughly the form that it took under their guidance.

One of the forces has already been identified – the suppression of a new generation by an older generation (and, to add insult to injury, by a generation which had made such a song and dance about 'youth'). But other, socio-economic, factors need to be drawn into the picture. Especially in the UK, rising unemployment and general economic stagnation gave the Punks'

Below: Punks at a King's Cross pub, London, 1987. Photo: Gavin Watson.

Right: Late 1970s London Punk couple. Politics and surrealism share a space on the man's T-shirt, which juxtaposes the message 'We Are All Prostitutes' with a photograph of a smiling Margaret Thatcher.

Below: Yuriko, a Japanese Punk, Shibuya, Tokyo, 1993. Photo: Yurie Nagashima.

nihilistic battle-cry of 'No Future!' a credible ring of truth. Culturally, too, things were at a low ebb: Abba was dominating the UK charts, with 'Mamma Mia' and 'Dancing Queen' both staying at number one for weeks on end. And, in the broader arts picture, it was a time lacking in creative flair and innovation, with two interesting exceptions – the 'Prostitution' exhibition, presented by Genesis P. Orridge and Cosey Fanni Tutti at the Institute of Contemporary Arts, which challenged the demarcation line between art and pornography, and 'The Rocky Horror Show', which celebrated the tackiest residues of popular culture – both of which took place in London and both of which explored territory which Punk would come to inhabit.

But, perhaps most importantly of all, by 1976 there was no denying the fact that the Age of Aquarius – which had seemed for almost a decade to be just over the horizon – was indefinitely on hold as the rock stars and other would-be saviours conferred with their accountants. The Punk generation grew up in the shadow of the Hippy's ever optimistic, utopian dream. When the sun set on this vision the only thing left was to set off with a cynical shrug in the opposite direction.

In this, the Punks must be seen as anti-Hippies. Think of the love-&-peace, longhaired, back-to-nature, smiling stereotype of the Hippy and then conjure up its photographic negative: sinister black leather, aggressive metal studs, perverse bondage trousers, Day-glo artifice and a snarl. Westwood, McLaren, Lou Reed, Iggy Pop, Richard Hell and Richard O'Brien may have been Punk's godparents but its real parents were none other than the Hippies, for it was they who constituted the thesis of Punk's angry antithesis.

This negative definition situation gave the early Punks a lot of room for manoeuvre. To appreciate the richness of their original diversity, let us time-travel back to an evening at Louise's nightclub, where the core group of London's Punks could be found inventing themselves in the seminal summer of '76.

One of the hundreds of London Punks who throughout the early 1980s engaged in a visual form of busking by posing for photographs in exchange for money from tourists.

Located on Poland Street in London's Soho, Louise's was a club for lesbians which had existed for many years before the Punks were led there by a few of their female members who were themselves lesbians or bisexual. Louise was an elegant Frenchwoman who, with her friend Francis Bacon, used to sit drinking champagne at a small table towards the rear of the club.

By the summer of '76 the 'Punks' (as they were now known) were often the dominant group at Louise's but their styles of dress were anything but homogeneous. A few wore fetishistic outfits in rubber or PVC – either from SEX or from the kinky 'glamourwear' firm She 'N' Me. Some wore deliberately battered school blazers with loose and dangling ties. Some wore see-through string vests or combinations of army surplus and cheap lingerie. There were a lot of leather jackets and some early experiments with 'tribal' hair and make-up. And yes, there were a few kids wearing the bin-liners, Dr Marten boots, ripped T-shirts, dog-collars, safety pins and tight drainpipes which would become the media's Punk stereotype. But many also flaunted the 'dressy' attire that would later be identified with the New Romantics.

At Louise's you could show up wrapped from head to toe in bandages or you could simply take some magnificently boring outfit like a cheap polyester suit and paint rude words all over it. There were surrealist convicts, tarty nuns, twenty-first-century prostitutes, mad Martians, bowler-hatted businessmen gone to seed and Hollywood-style Zulu chiefs. The only (unspoken) rule was that you couldn't get in if you looked like a Hippy: no denim, no beards, no shoulder-length hair, no peasant-style ethnic dress, no sandals, no bell-bottoms, no grandad vests and absolutely no 'Smiley' T-shirts. On a good night there were more creative styles packed into this little club than had been seen in all of London since at least the sixties.

Yet within just a few months the media had succeeded in reducing this sartorial anarchy to a stereotype. By 1977 there were kids fitting this fixed, limited identikit image materializing like B-movie monsters in just about every town and village in the UK. By 1978 such creatures were to be found throughout the USA. Within a decade they had invaded Japan, Western Europe, Eastern Europe and even Russia. The 'Media Punk' was a kind of virus – transmitted by the very newspaper, magazine and television reports which sought to warn the world of the Punk Menace.

Predictably, these mutant replicants made pilgrimages to the King's Road where they discovered that SEX had become Westwood's 'World's End' (prefiguring the rise of the New Romantics). But by now there were plenty of small shops eager to satisfy their sartorial needs. Up until the end of the eighties they would also have found a relatively prosperous contingent of British Punks making a living by posing for photographs for tourists in a sort of visual version of busking (reflecting the fact that they had become Britain's foremost tourist attraction). The hair, make-up and clothing of both the natives and the pilgrims had grown ever more flamboyant but they were basically variations on the stereotype created by the media from the original Punks' wide range of stylistic experimentation.

And so it came to pass that Punk ended up being shaped most profoundly by those two groups which its members most despised – first the Hippies, then the media. Yet it must also be said that the Punks had the last laugh. By the end of the seventies many a thirty-plus, longhaired, Leftover Hippy had found that his cushy job in music or media had been handed over to some spiky-haired youth. Punk accomplished exactly what it set out to do: the demolition of that numbing status quo which passed for 'alternative culture' in the mid-seventies.

In the process Punk changed the world – arguably more so than any other single styletribe before or since. Ushering in postmodernism before its time, Punk was amazingly eclectic, drawing stylistic inspiration from sources as diverse as the Rockers (motorbike jacket), the Skinheads (DMs) and even the Psychedelics (artificial colours) but blending these into a totally original concoction.

In part this originality stemmed from Punk's insistence that (as with music) style should be based on a DIY approach which generated endless, bizarre variety. Then, too, the kinds of garments and adornments which Punk threw together were themselves more often than not so unsuited to each other (so like the Surrealists' chance encounter on an operating table of a sewing machine and an umbrella) that a coherent synthesis was never on the cards. The result: a permanent streetstyle revolution which would explode into myriad subgroups and bring a breathtaking quickening of pace.

The French use the word *bricolage* to refer to an act of creation which cobbles together existing, 'found', often unrelated bits and pieces. It is an appropriate label for what was unique and revolutionary about Punk style. Whereas all previous styletribes had chosen their sources of inspiration with an obvious historical logic, the Punks just grabbed whatever caught the eye.

Such sartorial anarchy was (and is) central to Punk style/ideology, and it is also this quality which arguably has most directly influenced mainstream style and fashion. From the early eighties right up to the present day, only the 'fashion victim' has worn a head-to-toe outfit from one design source. Instead, we strive to combine the seemingly uncombinable and to do so in a way which demonstrates our own personal, amateur involvement. It is this, rather than ripped frocks held together with safety pins, which constitutes Punk's true legacy.

Emulating the original 'Catwoman' (a founder member of the Proto-Punks and an important stylistic innovator), this London Punk has duplicated the same look in a tattoo.

Above: 1980 mail order ad for Punk clothing and accessories. Like many Punks, the creators of this look – Jane Kahn and Patty Bell – would embrace a very different style in the New Romantic era (see page 95).

new romantics

Punk caught the media off guard. Attentions were focused elsewhere and the average journalist was too old to spot the anger and frustration which was building among young people throughout the mid-seventies. But once the realization grew that items about Punks sold newspapers and magazines and pushed up television ratings, youthculture once again became the media's pet subject.

The only trouble was that after a while the Punks began to lose the ability to shock. And, at least in Britain, as Crazy Colour and spiky hair became a common sight, the media began to feel the need for a new, even more newsworthy, styletribe.

There were, in fact, several candidates – 'cults', in the parlance of the day – already available. For example, there were the *Young*

Above: Some of the original, founder members of 'The Cult With No Name', photographed by the author at the Blitz club, London, in 1980.

Right: Vivienne Westwood influenced the New Romantics as much as she had influenced the Punks. Here, some of her clothes are modelled on the steps of her World's End shop by style innovator and club organizer Philip Sallon.

Right: Patty Bell and Jane Kahn, whose small shop Kahn & Bell in the Great Gear Market (King's Road, London) served in the early 1980s as a key meeting place for New Romantics as well as a source of distinctive, imaginative garments.

Far right: Couple at the 'People's Palace' evening at the Rainbow Theatre in Finsbury Park, London, 1980.

Soul Rebels[1] who looked sharp in their American-style sportswear which they blended with glam/Funk elements and who (unlike the Northern Soulies) sought to show that new forms of soul music were evolving with the times. But the fact that these Young Soul Rebels were predominantly black kept the media's interest to a minimum and rendered this interesting subculture almost invisible outside its own immediate environment. Also, in the mid to late seventies a large number of young British Rockabillies – 'Cats' – were to be seen prowling the streets of London. But (perhaps sensing that American-inspired nostalgia could never step into Punk's chunky footsteps) the media did not give these the space which was appropriate to their numbers.

What did catch the media's attention was the emergence of the half-Skinhead, half-Punk, Oi!s, who always seemed willing to oblige with a provocative (sometimes racist) quote and a menacing snarl to the camera. Here was a styletribe which the media could get its teeth into but, on the other hand, not

one whose story was ever going to amuse and entertain. Nor was it one in which the British could take pride. No, what was needed was a predominantly white, zany but politically inoffensive, flamboyant, overdressed styletribe which would provoke wry chuckles of disbelief rather than serious concern. Happily, by late 1978, the blueprint was already off the drawing board.

Since the earliest days of Punk there had always existed within its ranks an energetic little clique of self-proclaimed Posers who took more interest in dressing up and clubbing than in formulating an ideology of anarchic revolution. Invariably showing up in the most inventive creations, the key members of this group – people like Philip Sallon, George O'Dowd, Steve Strange and Chris Sullivan – had been well received at Louise's (the lesbian club in Soho which had doubled as a Punk meeting place). But as Punk tended more and more towards a stereotyped uniformity and as the 'Hard Punks' (like the 'Hard Mods' before them) turned their backs on fancy dress, these exquisite Posers were

increasingly left out in the cold. When Louise's closed in 1978 and this became literally the case, it was time for them to find both a new home and a new direction.

Or perhaps an *old* direction – as what was required would clearly have to be pre-Punk in origin. And, given the preoccupations of the Posers, it would need to be glamorous and experimental in terms of gender definition. Accordingly, Rusty Egan, Steve Strange and Chris Sullivan took over a little club in Soho called Gossips for one night a week. They called it 'Bowie Night'.

This event heralded a new development in club culture as well as the launch of a new styletribe. Instead of taking place on a Friday or Saturday when all kinds of nine-to-five types might lower the tone of the proceedings, Bowie Night was held on Tuesdays. Furthermore, the music, ambience and choice of customer was controlled by streetsmart kids rather than an out-of-touch club owner.

In this way, the 'one nighter' revolutionized London club life and set the stage for a 'narrow-casting' of tastes and interests which

Above: **Milliner Steven Jones, pictured in a New Romantic London club early in the 1980s. Note how his style, which changed weekly, could be seen in this instance as a precursor of the Goths.**

Below right: **George O'Dowd (Boy George), prior to achieving fame with Culture Club, in an early New Romantic club in London, 1980.**

in its specificity would promote the rise of dozens of small 'cults'.

When Bowie Night grew too big for Gossips, Egan and Strange switched to a larger club called the Blitz, which was decorated with Second World War posters ordering you to grow more vegetables. Despite the décor, the place attracted huge queues of bizarrely attired Posers all desperately hoping that Steve Strange – who guarded the door like St Peter – would let them in. Hot on their heels were the media pundits – pleased as punch that at last a suitable replacement to the Punks had been found but unable to come up with a name for them other than the 'Cult With No Name'.

For a time, the members of London's latest styletribe became known as 'Blitz Kids', after the name of the club. However, the inappropriateness of this was underlined when a string of other one-nighter clubs opened to cater to the same crowd on different nights of the week. Then, suddenly, the media began to favour the label 'New Romantics'. Although some of us might have preferred 'Posers', New Romantics did conjure up vivid images of soft, extravagant fabrics, elegance and finery. And whether they were Ziggy Stardust-inspired futurists in silver lamé or 1930s nostalgia-inspired sophisticates in white tuxedos and evening gowns, what the New Romantics had in common and what separated them from the Punks was an addiction to the glamorous.

Despite the fact that the New Romantics were themselves more often than not kids who had fallen loosely within Punk's broad domain, they now emerged in a sense as anti-Punks, substituting the elegant for the slovenly, the precious for the vulgar, Dressing Up for Dressing Down. Such a reversal is hardly unique in the history of streetstyle but what is astonishing is that it should have been accomplished within just a couple of years.

This happened in part because the original Posers were the ultimate quick-change artists, but perhaps even more because the emergence of Punk had whetted the media's appetite for identifying and promoting new, rapidly changing streetstyle cults. A club of Blitz Kids having fun dressing up was in fact transformed by the media into a fully fledged, international subculture defined by a philosophy of 'new romanticism' which always seemed a bit of an afterthought.

But is this cynical assessment really accurate? Among the New Romantics were hundreds of talented clothing designers, musicians and club entrepreneurs who never quite fulfilled their promise in the straight-jacket of Punk but who now forged a link between streetstyle, club culture and popular music which remains in effect to this day. They also possessed formidable PR skills. Indeed, perhaps the greatest accomplishment of the New Romantics was the extent to which they brought the media within their own control – prompting the launch of a new breed of 'style magazines' such as *i-D* and *The Face* which, for the first time, gave club culture and streetstyle the credit they deserve.

Right: Club organizer Anna Goodman dressed in clothes from the shop Symphony of Shadows, which in 1982, when the photo was taken, was located in London's Hyper Hyper market.

Far right: The logo from the author's membership card for the original Batcave club, 1981.

goths

By 1981, the British generation which had entered adolescence with Glam, learned to dance with Northern Soul, and become in turn the Punks and the New Romantics was in something of a quandary. They had become the victims of their own inventiveness. British pop musicians, clothing designers, videomakers, photographers, journalists and club entrepreneurs had conquered the world but (just as in the mid-sixties) commercial success had been achieved at the expense of meaningful subcultural identity. In particular, the New Romantics – always more a fancy–dress party than a tribe – were being sucked into the pop and fashion industries to such an extent that street credibility was in short supply.

The time had come for something with little mainstream commercial potential. Accordingly, a small clique decided to paint it black. In a sense this was nothing new. The

Punks had exulted in nihilism, and romanticism – new or old – could not exist without a chill of foreboding and a recognition of death's dark shadow. But now it was time to accentuate the negative, turn one's back on gaiety and go Gothic.

As fate would have it, the club which officially marked this transformation – the Batcave – opened in 1981 in the same venue, Gossips, that had hosted Bowie Night and thereby launched the New Romantics four years earlier. And, significantly, the ghost of Bowie and his Glam(orous) confederates still lurked in the corners. While the New Romantics contributed fancy-dress nostalgia and the Punks a kinky nihilism, Glam's contribution – as ever – was a refusal to accept traditional restrictions on the definition of masculinity.

The Batcave brought all these elements together and the result was Goth: a profusion of black velvets, lace, fishnets and leather

tinged with scarlet or purple, accessorized with tightly laced corsets, gloves, precarious stilettos and silver jewelry depicting religious and occult themes. Hair was jet black, backcombed to reach the stars. Faces were pancaked to deathly white with eyes and lips slashed with blood-red or black. All of it for males as often as for females.

What at the time seemed like just another transitory cult has had remarkable staying power. To this day, more than a decade on from the Batcave, even the smallest, most isolated village in Britain seems to have a couple of young Goths huddling protectively together.

Part of the reason for this has already been mentioned. To a majority which fetishizes happiness, Goth is by its very nature off-putting and therefore it has avoided the fate of being drawn into the mainstream. Thus, whereas a much imitated styletribe like, for example, the Skaters has

Right: Patricia Morrison, bass guitarist, ex-Gun Club, ex-Sisters of Mercy, and now solo artist, pictured in 1984 in a lace and rhinestone outfit designed by herself. Photo: Christina Birri.

Below: Standing in line for the Batcave club, early 1980s.

had constantly to chop and change in order to keep one step ahead of its trendy imitators, the Goths (like Dracula) have had the luxury of timelessness.

Perhaps, too, Goth's longevity derives from the essential appeal of its attitude and vision. While the majority may seek fun and frivolity, there always seems to be a minority – especially among angst-ridden youth – who are comforted by and attracted to a romanticized, stylish vision of life in the shadow of death. Since the Batcave's inhabitants first began to be seen on Britain's streets, the public has been perplexed by this contingent of 'Glad To Be Doomed Youth'. But are they not simply the modern heirs to a tradition which is at least as old as Byron and Shelley? (How amusing to imagine these old romantics time-travelling to an early night at the Batcave or, more recently, to an evening at the Slimelight club or a get-together of the Vampyre Society!) But it isn't all doom and gloom: to this older, more serious foundation is often added a macabre sense of humour, evident in a fascination with the 1950s American cartoonists Charles Addams and Edward Gorey and with cult American TV

Right: Gothically attired members of the Vampyre Society on a 1992 outing to Whitby, Yorkshire – a key location of Bram Stoker's original *Dracula*.

Below: Fashion designer John Galliano in Gothic mood – from his Spring/Summer 1992 collection. Photo: Niall McInerney.

Below right: Goth style displayed at the Slimelight club, London, 1983.

shows of the 1960s such as *The Addams Family* and *The Munsters*.

Inevitably, despite the Goths' initial success in forging a sense of communality and subcultural identity, they have in time developed internal schisms. The 'Gothics' – resplendent in superbly crafted, often historically accurate nineteenth-century costumes – view the common-or-garden Goths as rather scruffy and, well, punkish. In addition, both these groups show contempt for the 'Saturday Goths', who dress up only for special events and have little philosophical/mystical involvement.

Yet, at least from an outsider's perspective, compared to most post-Punk subcultures the Goths/Gothics seem remarkably coherent as a group – linked forever in the tender comradeship of the un-dead, finding sustenance in the poignancy of their fate.

Left and above: Young Casuals in East London in 1983. Photos: David Corio.

casuals

Like the streetcorner, the nightclub and the music gig, the football terrace is a place where streetstyles are born and bred. At least, this is true in Britain, where the football stadium has long been a place where (predominantly working-class) males forge a communal identity which goes far beyond that of fans rooting for a particular team. Although men of all ages participate, it is the young who have most successfully translated such allegiance into a recognizable visual style.

It was on the football terraces that the Skinheads first appeared in mass in the late 1960s. By the late seventies, however, a very different look began to emerge. While the

Skinheads had used their dress to show pride in their proletarian origins, this new style proclaimed personal success and wealth by means of prominent, upmarket labels like Lacoste, Inega, Lois and Burberry. But though a world away from the Skinheads' rough-and-ready (but always immaculately polished) 'bovver boots', this new style was also in the same Skinhead/Hard Mod tradition that had made a cult of pristine Fred Perry sportshirts.

The 'Casuals', as they came to be known early in the eighties, had crystallized in all but name by the late seventies. Great controversy still rages regarding precisely where this occurred. In his July 1983 article in *The Face*,

Ushering in a long overdue British menswear revolution

'The Ins and Outs of High Street Fashion',[1] Kevin Sampson makes what seems like a convincing case for locating their origins in the impoverished (yet mysteriously satellite-dished) Scotland Road area of Liverpool. According to Sampson, the young 'Scallies' (slang for Liverpudlians) who came from this area began 1977 with Punkish inclinations, picked up on the wedge-style haircut which David Bowie displayed on the cover of *Low* and then quickly shifted into expensive sportswear and a more 'football oriented lifestyle' early in 1978.

Other sources insist that the look originated among the 'Perries' of nearby Manchester or among various London football fans. But cutting across all this regional rivalry is a general point which is of greater significance.

The success of British football in Europe during this period (and in the early eighties) encouraged a great many fans to attend away games on the Continent. Contact with supporters there, especially in Italy and France – where stadiums have long been filled with men who look as if they have just stepped off a fashion catwalk – made the British determined to smarten up their act. If Britain could produce first-class footballers, why should their fans look second-class? So the British balance of payments plummeted into the red as Lacoste, Fila, Ellesse and Christian Dior laughed all the way to the bank.

Nor, I think, can one overlook the fact that the rise of the Casuals precisely matched the rise of Margaret Thatcher. Indeed, weren't the former the ultimate expression of the latter's philosophy? Pulling themselves up by their bootstraps by dint of cunning enterprise, always flying the flag, giving short shrift to the liberals and moaning minnies, the Casuals gave Thatcherism its most literal interpretation.

Their golden age ended, however, before the Iron Lady was shown the door. Some say it was the coming of rave and too much Ecstasy which distracted the Casuals from their perfection of sportswear chic. Others point to the tragedy which took place at the Haysel Stadium in Belgium in 1985 and which brought to an end the Casuals' sporting/shopping expeditions on the Continent.

Though I find it hard to generate much affection for the Casuals (aside from the violence, did their creativity ever extend much beyond an eye for the expensive?), it must be said that their influence has been great. Not only did they propel rave on its way, they also paved the way for the phenomenal success of firms like Chipie, Chevignon, Diesel and Soviet in the 1990s. More than this, however, they ushered in a long overdue British menswear revolution. That sharpness of style and consummate attention to detail which characterized the early Mods (and, it should be said, many Skinheads) had been lost in the late seventies. Like the Mods before them, the Casuals turned Britain on to quality European menswear and, in their own way, helped to make men more open to the pleasures of narcissism.

Above: **Details from mid-1980s Casual wear which underline this subculture's addiction to labels. Photos: Justin Alphonse.**

psychobillies

Paul Fenech, lead singer and founder member of The Meteors. Photo: Paul Slattery.

Psychobillies Joe and Ray at the Dunstable Tattoo Festival in 1991. Photo: John DeCastro.

At first glance it is hard to imagine a more unlikely combination than Punk and Rockabilly, but the Psychobillies made a virtue of such apparent incompatibility. At the wonderfully named 'Klub Foot', the West London venue where the Psychobillies first came together as a subculture, their fusion of 1950s Americana and 1970s British Punk seemed both obvious and inevitable.

To make the connection one must forget the soft drizzle of sentimentality which in the end became all too typical of the Rockabillies (Elvis singing about Teddy Bears in Vegas) and go back to the angry, licentious snarl of their early days. From this perspective it is clear that the thumping beat, the in-your-face sexuality, the deliberate shunning of prissy sophistication and the greasy quiffs of the early Rockabillies were in tune with Punk's gutsy spirit of raw rebellion. The Punks simply added a stylistic extremism, an assumption of gender equality and a fetishistic trashiness which could not conceivably have existed in Memphis in the mid-fifties. The common denominator is rock 'n' roll energy in its purest form.

Although the slezoid music and style of the American post-Punk band The Cramps was clearly an inspiration, the first 100-percent-proof Psychobilly band was The Meteors, which formed in South London in 1980. With musicians consisting of one Rockabilly, one Punk and one psychedelic horror enthusiast, The Meteors constituted a complete microcosm of the subculture which would almost immediately form around it.

By 1982, with the opening of Klub Foot, the Psychobillies were more than simply the followers of a cult band. Their style has been termed 'Mutant Rockabilly' and it is an apt description – with cartoon quiffs sometimes dyed green or purple and always thrust out far beyond the expectations of gravity, aggressive studded belts and Doc Martens, shredded, bleached jeans and leather jackets painted with post-nuclear-holocaust imagery. Here were creatures straight out of tacky comic books or ketchup-splattered horror movies brought to life (?) and waiting patiently for the last bus to Planet Zorch.

Needless to say, such an extreme styletribe never reached an enormous size and its bands (in time including the likes of Guana Batz, Demented Are Go, Batmobile and the truly unbelievable King Kurt) never appeared on TV's *Top of the Pops*. It did, however, quickly acquire members throughout most of Europe (especially Germany, Italy and Spain) and a large, dedicated following in Japan.

Stylistically, the Psychobillies' principal effect seems to have been on the Rockabillies – causing a shift towards battered denim workwear and away from fancy suits and pristine footwear. From there (and it should be remembered that the Rockabilly movement was huge in Britain in the early eighties) this look moved into the street-smart mainstream in the form of the 'Hard Times' look.

At one level the Psychobillies exhibited an alarming fixation with violence and wanton destruction, but this was always tempered by a wonderful, surreal sense of humour, which made you smile, even as you crossed hurriedly to the other side of the street.

Right: Latex shorts and bra top from Ectomorph, Krystina Kitsis's design company, which was one of the first to introduce rubber fetishism into fashion in the mid-1980s. Photo: Wilfred Moulin.

Fetishism is nothing new. Many tribal peoples believe that inanimate objects can possess inexplicable powers. Portugese explorers in the fifteenth century called such objects 'feitico' – meaning charming. This later became 'fetish' and in the late nineteenth century Krafft-Ebbing, Binet and Freud made use of the word to describe objects which possess a sexual power which can rival or eclipse the erotic power of the human body.

Although a particular individual can develop a fetishistic attraction to practically any object, certain styles of dress have become more broadly categorized in this way – tightly laced corsets, stockings and suspenders, and stiletto heels, for example. In 1960s Swinging London, fetishistic or 'kinky' clothes in leather or PVC had wide appeal. This was particularly evident in *The Avengers* TV series in which Honor Blackman or Joanna Lumley would appear each week in a yet sexier, more futuristic catsuit.

Many of these garments were created by a designer called John Sutcliffe, who ran a small company called Atomage. When television and mainstream fashion moved away from their dalliance with 'kinky gear', Sutcliffe continued his work for private clients, making ever more bizarre creations. At the same time a range of obscure little magazines like *Pussy Cat* and *Relate* (with its 'Rubber Wife of the Month' feature) were catering to the same group of fetishistically inclined 'enthusiasts'.

But, except for the work of the artist Allen Jones, this world remained essentially underground and furtive until Malcolm McLaren and Vivienne Westwood brought it into the public eye with the launch of their shop 'SEX'. There, explicitly 'pervy' items were sold openly and provocatively. By this means (and with the discovery of the PVC 'glamourwear' firm She 'N' Me) fetishism became a central component of Punk iconography.

Above: Three revellers at the opening night of the first Skin Two club in Soho, London. The couple pictured above are fashion designers Lesley Beaumont and Daniel James.

pervs

Right: Pervy clubber, London, early 1980s.

Far right: Slashed Latex bodysuit by Pam Hogg. Autumn/Winter 1992/93 collection. Photo: Niall McInerney.

The Goths continued the Punks' interest in fetishism and translated it into a more dressy, extravagant style – as is evident in the visual evolution of the Punk/Goth group Siouxsie & the Banshees. Groups like Soft Cell and Frankie Goes To Hollywood brought fetishistic imagery further within the pop music mainstream. Popular culture has always veered between the natural and the perverse. In the seventies the Leftover Hippies had sought to cling to the former but were overruled by the Punks. In the early eighties a glance at *Top of the Pops* demonstrated the extent to which popular culture was eagerly carrying on in the Punks' kinky stiletto footsteps.

The early eighties in London was also a time which saw strange new 'one-nighter' theme clubs opening on an almost weekly basis. These celebrated everything from the cult TV series *Thunderbirds* to Japanese experimental music. Late in 1983 a trend-spotting actor and his clothing designer girlfriend (both of whom have since found

fame and fortune in popular TV and wish to remain anonymous) started a new, one-nighter called 'Skin Two' in a little backstreet club in London's Soho.

This was the first attempt to bring together 'real fetishists' (from clients of Atomage to members of the Mackintosh Society) and the growing 'pervy' contingent within pop music and alternative clothing design. No one at the opening night of Skin Two (myself included) expected this daring venture to last more than a few weeks. History, however, has proved us wrong.

From a Monday night club which held, at most, a couple of hundred leather/rubber/PVC clad 'Pervs', a huge international subculture has grown. Today there are dozens of high-circulation glossy magazines, countless packed-out clubs and hundreds of successful fetish-oriented clothing designers established in Europe (notably Germany, France and Holland, as well as Britain), the USA, Australia and Japan. This 'fetish scene' is arguably the largest, most far-reaching and

Left: 'Warrior Women' Vein and Fran wearing clothes designed by Vein for Pagan Metal, London, 1993. Photo: Housk Randall.

Opposite left, and below: Sybille modelling Murray & Vern for the Skin Two 3 Collection, 1993. Photos: Peter Ashworth.

influential of any contemporary street- or club-based subculture.

Because the Pervs have exerted such a strong influence on mainstream culture via the extraordinary popularity of 'fetish fashion', it sometimes seems that superficiality has triumphed over substance. This is true up to a point, but it must also be said that beneath the Pervs' shiny black facade there is a serious commitment to exploring a new sexuality – one which seeks to replace the casual 'Your place or mine' promiscuity of the 1960s 'sexual revolution' with an approach that is more relationship-based, and more ritualistic (even spiritual). In the process, the Pervs are redefining and extending the meaning of sex itself.

At the same time the Pervs propose a way round the contemporary impasse of male/female power struggles by substituting instead Sub(missive)/Dom(inant) roles which are not specifically defined by gender. While this aspect of the Pervs' ideology addresses issues which have been raised by generations of feminists, the shift away from 'casual sex' takes seriously the reality of AIDS.

Through all of this 'The Pervy World' taps into the spirit of our age. It shouldn't surprise us, therefore, that this subculture and its look have had such widespread influence on both fashion and streetstyle. For example, within a wide spectrum of post-rave spin-off groups (most noticeably, the Technos), materials like rubber or PVC and styles which are clearly derived from an S/M iconography have lost all vestiges of stigma – becoming instead 'adjectives' which proudly proclaim pervy inclinations.

What was once limited to the clandestine activities of the middle-aged has become an accepted part of youth-oriented exhibitionistic club culture from Berlin to Sidney. This popularity shouldn't surprise us: AIDS, gender-related issues and a growing awareness of the deficiencies of the last 'sexual revolution' in the 1960s all point to the need for a new approach to erotic and sexual experience.

Run DMC, New York, 1988. The first rap group to find real success in the music charts, Run DMC were also the first to bring B-Boy style to mainstream attention. In particular, their huge hit 'My Adidas' provided this blossoming subculture with a visual icon. Photo: Janette Beckman.

b-boys & flygirls

From the moment in 1976 when Punk was born, kicking and screaming, the world's eyes focused (in disbelief) on Britain. Except for the hyped-up distraction of 'disco', the UK's virtual monopoly of popular culture continued well into the eighties as the visual flare of Britain's New Romantic pop musicians coincided with the MTV-led 'video revolution'. But, also in 1976, invisible to the outside world, the impoverished South Bronx of NYC was beginning to fashion a new, exciting youthculture under the banner of 'rap music' and 'hip-hop'.

In the best streetstyle tradition the location from which this movement sprang was literally the street. Jamaican DJs living in New York (most famously, Kool Herc) had brought with them the Kingston tradition of raucous street parties organized around competing sound systems. Their crews and these events became the focus of South Bronx streetlife. As in Jamaica, the DJ was king. Not content simply to play records, the likes of Grandmaster Flash took a more hands-on approach in which turntables were themselves played like musical instruments – 'scratching' over selected tracks and 'mixing' together often completely different sounds.

The result was dance music of the highest order which encouraged hundreds and then thousands of New York ghetto kids to perfect what became known as 'break-dancing' – letting rip on the instrumental 'breaks' between verses in a highly competitive fashion reminiscent of ancient African traditions in which participants, especially the men, tried to 'dance' each other off the floor.

Left: Rap artist Slick Rick, providing a definitive example of the use of adornment as a demonstration of wealth and success, 1990.
Photo: Janette Beckman.

Right: Both stylistically and musically, the early Flygirls typically let the B-Boys take the lead. In 1987 Salt 'N' Pepa – bright, bold, street, chic and fresh – changed all that.
Photo: Janette Beckman.

Below: Afrocentric style, as worn by A Tribe Called Quest, New York, 1990.
Photo: Janette Beckman.

Such dancers became known as 'B-Boys' (the 'B' short for 'break') or 'Flygirls' ('fly' being street slang for well-dressed, attractive, sexy). Despite the fact that American attentions were focused on Britain and the emerging rap musicians were given absurdly little air-play, 'The Message' (in Grandmaster Flash's phrase) eventually got through. The new music, the acrobatic break-dancing and the innovative graffiti art, which also derived from poor areas of New York, all added up to a dynamic subcultural force.

However, at least in the early days, such innovations in music, dance and art were not matched by the emergence of an equally distinctive new appearance style. Most of the new breed of rap musicians dressed (at least on stage) in a way which was derivative of OTT Funk. However, slowly but surely, the anonymous B-Boys and Flygirls evolved a style of their own. The essential ingredients were defined by the rigours of strenuous dancing: athletic trainers and tracksuits, together with snug caps which offered some protection during headspins.

Although rooted in the practical and the casual, the B-Boy style was also aspirational, relying (like the Casuals in Britain) on prominent upmarket labels. To these were added gold jewelry – huge, chunky necklaces or 'Dukie Ropes' culminating in gleaming enormous dollar signs – and, in time, tightly cropped hairstyles featuring amazingly intricate razored designs. The look was as 'street' as any look can be and when Run DMC had an enormous hit in 1986 with 'My Adidas' it was cemented into international

Above: **Break-dancer displaying original B-Boy style at the Roxy, New York, 1981. Photo: David Corio.**

Below: **Militant style, as worn by Public Enemy, London, 1987. Photo: David Corio.**

popular culture in a way which left little doubt that New York (and therefore the USA) had finally elbowed Britain aside.

Suddenly the B-Boys and Flygirls' style was the most copied in the world. To the chagrin of millions of parents, every kid simply had to own a pair of expensive trainers and a label-festooned hooded sports-top or tracksuit. Nor was this look limited to youngsters. Overnight it became the accepted uniform of trendy advertising executives and media moguls from LA to London.

As is inevitably the case with such unwanted emulation, the real B-Boys and Flygirls had no choice but to keep moving on – using new styles and labels to define their genuine subcultural identity and generating a whole string of distinctive styles which matched rap music's own evolution.

Firstly, beginning around 1987, the Paid In Full look of Erik B. & Rakim or Ultramagnetic MCs took the basic ingredients of B-Boy style and smartened them up by emphasizing the most chic brands of sportswear (Louis Vuitton, Gucci) and by taking gold accessories to a new extreme. The effect was less 'street' (no sane person would break-dance on the sidewalk in such expensive outfits) and more like Olympic athletes in designer sportswear displaying their victors' medallions with pride.

Next, circa 1988, came the Militant look which befitted the increasingly committed stance of groups like Public Enemy and BDP & KRS-1. As its name suggests, the predominant theme was 'urban commando chic' – black or camouflage pattern clothes set off with dazzlingly white, big-tongued trainers and, again, heavy gold jewelry.

The Afrocentric look which became prominent late in the eighties reflected rap's renewed determination to assert black cultural identity and roots. Effectively blending sportswear with traditional African fabrics (such as batik) and loose, comfortable styles, this look is exemplified by groups such as Jungle Brothers, Lakim Shabazz and Queen Latifah.

Significantly, in line with the political stance which lay behind this style, gold jewelry (which might have come from South Africa) was replaced with Afrikan medallions made of leather in the red, gold and green of the Ethiopian flag.

Although such styles first appeared and flourished in a historical sequence, they all continue to exist side by side to the present day – making the subculture which the B-Boys and Flygirls founded richly textured, dynamic and, to use the word which has become synonymous with this group, 'fresh'.

Ragga Boys hanging out in Kingston, Jamaica, in 1993. Photo: David Corio.

I n October of 1980 Michael Manley's Jamaican socialist experiment came to an abrupt end when Edward Seaga was elected Prime Minister. In tune with Reaganism in America and Thatcherism in Britain, this shift to the right was reflected in significant changes in popular culture in general and music and appearance styles in particular.

Manley's government had cultivated effective links with the Rastafarian cause. As Dick Hebdige points out in *Cut 'N' Mix*

He had invited [Haile] Selassie to the island for a state visit in 1966. In election campaigns, Manley had used the language of the Bible to win people's votes. He had stressed the link between the socialist tradition and the Rastafarian search for justice and a spiritual home. After all, wasn't socialism rooted in the same quest for justice and equality that had inspired the Rastafarians?[1]

In this sense, the collapse of Manley's socialism was also a blow to Rastafarianism.

Throughout the eighties a new generation of Jamaican youth – Seaga's Children, so to speak – used their music, their dance and their clothing styles to signpost their separateness from Rasta culture. Their music, which became known as Ragga, drew heavily on synthesized sounds and its often contentious ('slack') lyrics blatantly celebrated sex, violence and personal gain. Sexually provocative dances like the 'bogle', the 'Santa Barbara' and the 'Armstrong' left little to the imagination. And the same was true of the Ragga girls' startling see-through or slashed outfits and their 'batty-rider' shorts, which often revealed more than they concealed. At the same time, the men's distinctive 'click suits', made of an intricate patchwork of shredded or stonewashed denim decorated with appliqué or rich

raggamuffins & bhangra style

raggamuffins & bhangra style **109**

brocade – although 'Raggamuffin' by name – conveyed a message that was one of success and wealth.

All of which could not possibly have been more at odds with Rastafarian style and values. Instead of using their appearance to show respect for the natural, the Raggamuffins flaunted gaudy artifice. Instead of Rasta 'I-an-I' humility, they boasted of individual success. Instead of the Rasta woman's chaste concealment came the Ragga girl's provocative display of flesh.

While the Raggamuffin's focus on power and wealth might be seen as a throwback to the pre-Rasta days of the Rude Boys, again, their style was contradictory. As we have seen, the Rude Boys' look was characterized by a tight, trim, understated restraint. Raggamuffins of both sexes, on the other hand, are glitzy, ostentatious – 'extra' in the extreme.

What began in the 'dancehall' subculture of Downtown Kingston spread like wildfire to Miami, New York and, of course, London, where Ragga musicians like Shabba Ranks and General Levy performed for sell-out crowds of female fans bogling their batty-

riders and male fans eyeing the layered patchwork of each other's 'click suits'.

Whatever criticism might be made of Ragga's provocative 'slackness' and violent inclinations (both of which are arguably more than matched by some factions within rap and heavy metal), Raggamuffin clothing and adornment style is refreshingly unique. In particular, its layered textures – juxtaposing velvet, lace, fishnet, appliqué, leather, suede, brocade, Lycra, ruffles and many different shades of denim – constitute a revolutionary approach to fabric design which is already being copied in high fashion.

Like the Rastafarians and the Rude Boys before them, the Raggamuffins once again demonstrate Jamaica's extraordinary ability to create new, innovative streetstyles which the rest of the world finds irresistible.

One especially interesting example of Ragga's influence is the way in which it has fused with Asian Bhangra. Little known outside Asian communities until the late eighties, Bhangra is an ancient folk music which has increasingly incorporated Western popular music and instruments. As such, it expresses the dual loyalties facing the young

British Asians who take pride in their own cultural roots but also recognize that they are part of a broader Western culture.

Despite enormous sales, Bhangra music has rarely been seen on *Top of the Pops* or *The Chart Show*. While huge groups of Asian young people were flocking to Bhangra concerts (typically held in the afternoon to avoid traditional night curfews for girls) the rest of Britain remained largely oblivious. What has changed this – and at the same time created new, dynamic possibilities – is the way some of those within Bhangra have forged a link with Ragga music and style.

It was, of course, the urban proximity of Britain's Asian and West Indian communities which made such hybridization possible. For, despite the fact that the previous generation within both these communities have been somewhat wary of each other, today's Asian and West Indian youngsters have grown up together, learned from each other and recognized common concerns regarding white racism.

Typical of this background and these attitudes is the popular musician Apache Indian, who grew up in Handsworth in South

Yorkshire. He developed an early appreciation of his West Indian neighbour's reggae which intensified when this was transforming into Ragga. The result is a unique, exciting music which, though it may be recorded in Kingston, finds a warm reception among both young British Asians and Indians in India, where Apache Indian has become a pop phenomenon without equal.

Bhangra's 'muffinization' has at the same time influenced appearance styles. It used to be the case that Bhangra style was schizophrenically divided between the traditional Asian dress of its musicians and the current Western fashion of its young fans. But the ease with which Raggamuffin, rap and other black-derived style innovations are being interwoven with traditional Asian dress and garment industry expertise is turning the Bhangra scene into a place of visual as well as musical fusion.

With his razored hairstyle, his enormous gold chains and his Ragga-influenced garments, Apache Indian symbolizes a multi-cultural, multi-racial future, which hopefully represents the Britain of the twenty-first century.

Apache Indian wearing clothes by Cross Colours on his first album, *No Reservations,* in 1993.

new age travellers

Punk killed off the Hippies. Or so it seemed. Certainly you didn't hear much about them after the spiky-tops took centre stage. But in reality they had simply migrated to the country.

From the very beginning, as far back as 'The Summer of Love' in 1967, the Hippies' love of 'the natural' and their horror of 'the plastic' had pointed towards rural life. The commune portrayed in the 1969 film *Easy Rider* had thousands of real-life counterparts scattered across North America. In Britain the favoured locations were Wales, Cornwall and Scotland. After 1976 (the emergence of the Punks perhaps strengthening the Hippies' resolve to get out of town) these areas saw a final wave of longhaired immigrants determined to live off the land.

Of course this was only really possible for those Hippies who were rich enough to be able to buy arable land or who had welcoming friends on an established commune. For the not so lucky (or for all those who found they couldn't cope with a sedentary life), the only viable option was to become a Traveller.

Since time immemorial the gypsies, the tinkers and other groups had lived on the road and their lifestyle served as an obvious model for many a Hippy. Their ethnicity appealed to Folkie inclinations. Their migratory way of life mirrored the restlessness that had driven the Hippies' other predecessors, the Beats, *On the Road*. And the gypsies were the original alternative culture – always deliberately setting themselves apart from (and typically unwelcome within) mainstream society.

And so it came to pass that many a Hippy became a Traveller. The result was that their ramshackle (but usually well-cared-for) caravans became a common sight across Great Britain, and especially in the south of England. There were also whole communities of Travellers living in tent-like 'benders' made from hazel twigs or in native-American-style tepees.

The local authorities hated them and kept moving them on. But each summer the coherence and vitality of Britain's travelling tribes was reinforced by a series of free festivals, the most famous of which was the celebration of the summer solstice at Stonehenge.

Opposite: **Visitors to the Forest Fayre, Forest of Dean, Gloucestershire, 1993. Photo: Kate Owens.**

Below left: **Australian 'Freaks' after the Glastonbury Festival, 1993.** *Centre*: **Susie Franks and baby Sam at the UFO (Underground Freak Out) and Organon Festival in South Wales, 1991. Susie is wearing her own clothing and hat designs. Photo: Sandra Smith.** *Right*: **Hippy, Punk and Rasta influences in evidence at the Glastonbury Festival, 1993. Photo: Robbie Crow.**

All of which – the getting closer to nature, the New Age spiritualism, the ethnically inspired clothes, the long hair – were really just an extension of the Hippies' original subculture. It might have remained so, but for events which took place away from the idyllic countryside in the black heart of London. Throughout the seventies the Camden Town area of North London had become a 'free city' of squatters. When Camden Council began massive evictions of these squatters in the late seventies, tens of thousands of people decided to flee to the countryside. Significantly, a large number of these were of a Punkish persuasion.

Given the fact that (as we have seen) the Punk subculture was conceived in direct, angry opposition to the Leftover Hippies, one might have expected wariness, even conflict, when these ex-squatter Punks met up with the Travellers. On the contrary. Peace & love was typically the order of the day as both groups recognized the common denominator of their alternative values and their constant hassles from the authorities. The result was a remarkable mix of New Age spiritualism and 'No Future'/post-holocaust tribalism, of natural, folksy styles juxtaposed with Crazy-Coloured mohicans and 'bovver boots'.

Thus began a new age of New Age Travellers. Having established a common ground between two so radically different perspectives, the 'Hipunks' (as they might be called) were a remarkably invigorated and potent force. Throughout the early eighties more and more 'tribes' were established and more and more free festivals were added to an already busy summer social calendar.

But as the New(er) Age Travellers grew in numbers, it became increasingly clear that Margaret Thatcher's Britain would try to halt their advance. On 1 June 1985 a convoy of Travellers on their way to celebrate the summer solstice at Stonehenge were effectively ambushed by hundreds of police. They were forced into a field where vehicles were smashed, children taken into care and hundreds of arrests made. The 'Battle of the Beanfield' set the stage for a string of confrontations and evictions from common, unused land which continue to this day.

Despite such persecution the Travellers have flourished, keeping alive a vision of a New Age when urban dis-eases would be superseded and tribe-like communities could return to a more natural way of life. Although much of the media has painted a relentlessly negative 'dirty scroungers' image of the Travellers, many of their views (almost universally seen as crackpot only a few years ago) have been influential far beyond their subculture.

In particular, their concern for the environment has taken root throughout much of mainstream society, as is evident in the phenomenal rise of 'ecologically friendly' products and in the widespread support for pressure groups such as Greenpeace. Furthermore, these concerns have found stylistic expression in the clothing industries' 'Eco' movement. While some designers have switched to environmentally friendly materials and production processes, others, like the Belgian designer Martin Margiela, have developed 'deconstructionist' techniques whereby new styles are created from cut-up pieces of second-hand garments. In both instances an industry which has traditionally epitomized modern society's nonchalance regarding throwaway wastefulness is having to adjust to present and future realities.

Ironically, these ultimate outsiders – in keeping alive that respect for nature which first surfaced among the Folkies, the Surfers and the Hippies – have had a remarkable influence on 'normal society'. What began as just a bunch of Leftover Hippies, invigorated by contact with a bunch of Leftover Punks (and subsequently, as we shall see in a moment, a bunch of Leftover Ravers) has become a model for responsible, creative life in the twenty-first century.

Psychedelic, ethnic space rockers Ozric Tentacles, 1993.

Squatters demo, Trafalgar Square, London, 1993.

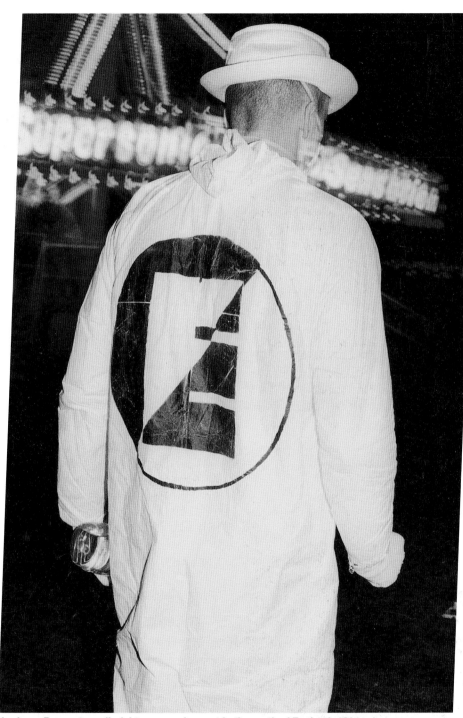

Hardcore Raver at an all-nighter open-air event in the north of England, 1991.
Photo: Steve Lazarides.

ravers

Ibiza was the only place to be in the Summer of 1985. A tiny Balearic island off the coast of Spain, it became the centre of the pop culture universe for one, or maybe two, summers. This wasn't because of its beaches or the delightful cobbled streets of its ancient capital. Ibiza's claim to fame was a string of huge and literally fantastic nightclubs like Ku, Pasha, Glory's and the appropriately named 'Amnesia' (which doesn't open until dawn) which were packed out with Europe's most devout hedonists.

It was all very mid-eighties Yuppie and yet at the same time flavoured by the carefree spirit of the Hippies who had invaded Ibiza in the sixties. 1985 was the summer when the drug Ecstasy and post-disco 'house music' (named after the gay Warehouse club in Chicago where it was created) became all the rage in Ibiza. Augmented by the bright, bold, casual yet sexy clothes on offer in Ibiza's many boutiques, it added up to a distinctive 'Balearic' lifestyle which would be influential for years to come.

In Britain, the summer but a fading memory, a group of Londoners resolved to inject the Ibizan spirit into an increasingly flagging club culture. First the Project Club and then Shoom offered Balearic/house rhythms, and as queues formed outside their doors, it became clear that this emerging 'acid house' subculture had a reality beyond holiday-fuelled exuberance.

In London – especially at Shoom – the Hippyish flavour of this new styletribe became evident as 'Smiley' T-shirts, tie-dyed, psychedelic patterns and peace & love became *de rigueur*. When one-off, typically illegal 'warehouse parties' – 'raves' – caught on, those dancing till dawn became known as

'Ravers'. Bringing together acid house music, Ecstasy, loose, dance-oriented clothes and Hippy vibes, this new subculture once again put Britain, and London, back at the centre of international youthculture.

All of which is a load of tripe if you happen to come from the north of England. From the perspective of Manchester or Liverpool, such goings-on in London or even Ibiza had precious little to do with the evolution of Rave culture.

Instead, the line of descent is traced back to the Scallies of Liverpool and the Perries of Manchester, who were now shifting away from the smart, cleancut Casual look which they had pioneered in the late 1970s towards a Tramp look which centred on enormous denim flares worn with hooded sports-tops, trainers and pageboy haircuts. These ex-Casuals called themselves 'Baldricks' (after a down-and-out character from the TV series *Blackadder*). They were typically working class, intensely regionalist and dismissive of everything that came from London.

They were also devoted football supporters and in this sense their brand of

Rave style must be seen as a logical extension of what had begun with the Casuals. Despite the jokey self-mockery of their name (the Baldricks), continued emphasis on brand labels such as the Manchester-based Joe Bloggs was clearly in the same aspirational, Dressing Up tradition. But significant changes from the classic Casual era were also in evidence and these were not limited to hairstyles and flares. In particular, the football terraces now competed with the dance floor at clubs like Manchester's Hacienda. And Ecstasy now competed with lager.

The effect of which was to bring the Scallies, the Perries and the Baldricks closer to the Ibiza-inspired Ravers of London. To be sure, Manchester (or 'Madchester' as it was now known) wasn't keen on the Hippyish, soft-centred ethos of the South (and this was reflected in the harder image of cherished Northern bands like the Stone Roses and the Inspiral Carpets). But in the context of huge raves like 'Sunrise', which drew kids from all over Britain, regional, stylistic and ideological distinctions were less apparent.

The differences between the Northern Baldrick-style Ravers and the Southern Shoom-style Ravers were always there ready to break through the surface. In practice, however, Ecstasy and the mesmerizing beat of acid house went a long way towards smoothing over regional rivalries and the Ravers became a homogeneous force without equal in Britain in the mid to late eighties. And when the police became ever more determined to stamp out illegal raves, the result was the realization that everyone had to pull together to demand 'The Right To Party'.

Nor did this spirit of ecumenism end at the limits of the Ravers' subculture. At the same time that raves were being shut down and sound systems confiscated, the Travellers were facing similar problems in staging their summer festivals and this, in time, led to a spirit of comradeship between these two very different groups.

The extraordinary nature of this union cannot be lightly dismissed. While it is true that the Shoom-derived Ravers displayed a great many Hippy-like qualities which at least superficially linked them with the Travellers, the Northern-based Ravers, with their roots in the football terraces, were as different from the Travellers as chalk from cheese. Furthermore, *all* the Ravers exulted in a party-on hedonism, a 'weekender' lifestyle and a love of psychedelic artifice which was at odds with the Travellers' full-time commitment to a responsible way of life in tune with nature and spiritual pursuits.

Nevertheless, despite the grumblings of many of the older Travellers, a reconciliation of sorts has been achieved. At the heart of this accord is the belief that The-Right-To-Party and The-Right-to-Hold-Festivals constitute a bottom line of personal freedom. In this sense, therefore, the heavy-handedness of Britain's successive Tory governments has had the effect of bringing together the most apparently incompatible of styletribes. Where once there were 'style wars' – between Mods and Rockers, Punks and Teds – there is now a spirit of common purpose which has already altered the nature and the course of streetstyle.

Below: 'Karma Collective' party – 'Boys Own' – early Summer, 1988. Photo: Cymon G. Eckel.
Below right: Ravers at the enormous 'Fantazia' festival at Castle Donington, Wiltshire, in 1993.

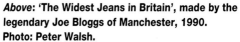

Above: 'The Widest Jeans in Britain', made by the legendary Joe Bloggs of Manchester, 1990. Photo: Peter Walsh.

Above centre: Ravers at a 'Land of Oz' evening at London's Heaven Club, 1989. Photo: David Swindells.

Above right: London, 1988 – 'The Future', one of the first 'acid house' events. Photo: David Swindells.

Right: Raving at the 'Roller Express'. Some classic Hardcore Ravers in Edmonton, North London, 1993. Photo: David Swindells.

London's Snap Club, 1988.
Photo: Adam Friedman.

Right: Rob Galliano, lead singer with Galliano, in deerstalker hat, at the *Straight No Chaser* Fifth Birthday Party in London, 1993.
Photo: Steve Lazarides.

Far right: 'Acid Jazz goes mainstream' at a trendy London club, 1991.
Photo: Adam Friedman.

acid jazz

Acciieeed!!! By 1988 this was the word on everyone's lips. It wasn't so much a drug as a state of mind. With youthculture in the grip of the 'Smiley' T-shirted Ravers and their hypnotic acid house music, suddenly anything which in another era would have been termed 'hot', 'cool', 'hip', 'fab' or 'far out' was instead preceded by the adjective 'acid'. It was hardly surprising, therefore, that when DJ Gilles Peterson wanted to wean his audience away from the monotony of house and turn them on to something new, he found himself labelling it 'Acid Jazz'.

What may have begun as a bit of a joke formed the basis of a dynamic and ever more influential subculture. Not only its name but also its success owed something to the omnipresence of rave and house in late-eighties Britain. Irritated by incessant hype and craving some 'real' (as opposed to synthesized) music, a small but determined clique focused their attentions on 'rare groove' – seeking out the obscure, under-appreciated music of other eras. While some got hooked on the seventies – Funk, in particular – others time-travelled further back to bebop and other experimental jazz styles of the late forties and fifties. Cross-fertilization between these diverse styles was only a matter of time.

But if the funkification of jazz now seems an obvious move, it was actually a long leap across two quite separate musical traditions. Funk had its roots in soul and R&B. Bebop, an earlier development, had arisen in counterpoint to swing's descent into overly orchestrated blandness. Not content with

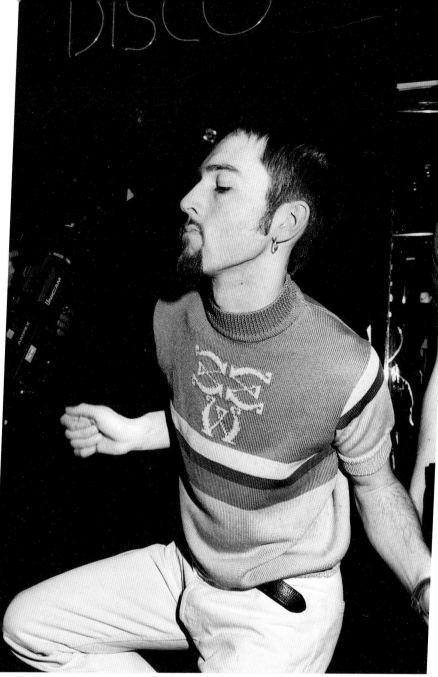

having brought together funk and experimental jazz, Gilles Peterson and his accomplices immediately set about throwing everything from mambo and salsa to 'dub' and rap into the Acid Jazz cocktail.

In keeping with this musical eclecticism, the clothing styles which developed within and around the Acid Jazz scene were inspired by amazingly diverse, even (one would have thought) contradictory sources. From the bebopping Hipsters came berets, goatees and sharp suits. From the Beatniks came a penchant for corduroy, beads and oversized black sweaters. Funk contributed seventies-style flares, wide-collar shirts, mock-crocodile loafers, dogtooth checks and leather or suede waistcoats. As the sounds of jazz awakened the original Mod spirit, Italian-inspired garments like suede-trimmed

A timeless package within which eighties Puma trainers share the dance floor with sixties tasselled loafers without a trace of incongruity

Gabicci cardigans were rediscovered. At the
same time the Skaters' Stussy and Pervert
T-shirts and the B-Boys' Kangol hats, Adidas
tracksuit tops and 'old school' trainers (Puma
States or Adidas Gazelles) caught on.

On the face of it, such eclectic styles
would seem to be unlikely partners and the
same can be said of Acid Jazz's diverse
musical ingredients. Certainly the Acid Jazz
scene has never achieved the uniform
homogeneity of, say, the Skinheads or even
the Zooties of the 1940s. This is a world
which emphasizes personal individuality in
both musical and visual taste.

It is only in comparison with other
contemporary styletribes that the coherence
of the Acid Jazzers becomes apparent. In
particular, as the Ravers plunged further and
further into their ecstatic but robotic frenzy,
Acid Jazz's pursuit of 'the real' became more
pronounced. Naturally, this claim to
authenticity hinged on the historic rootedness
of those musical and visual styles which
provided this subculture with a past.

Though never simply a revival and always
a unique synthesis, Acid Jazz is ever mindful
and respectful of its antecedents. This in itself
is hardly unique within the history of
streetstyle. (Indeed, quite the opposite.) What
is noteworthy about Acid Jazz is the
postmodern way in which it chooses to relate
to the past – nonchalantly jumbling together
different decades (the forties, the seventies,
the eighties) as well as radically different
styles (Bebop, Beatnik, Funk, Skater, B-Boy).
In this sense Acid Jazz represents
streetstyle's future: mixing and matching bits
of the past into a concoction which is
sometimes odd but always fresh and exciting.

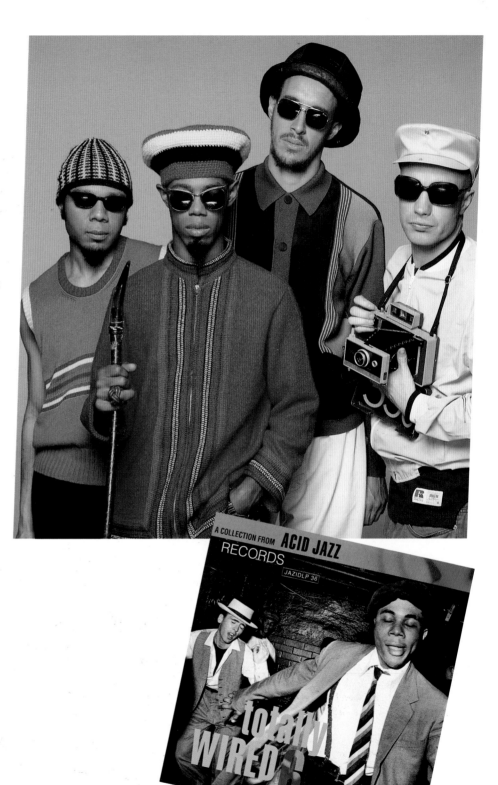

Above: Japanese Acid Jazz enthusiast at the *Straight No Chaser* Fifth Birthday Party in London, 1993. Photo: Steve Lazarides.

Right: Japanese jazz fan at Club Yellow, Tokyo, 1992. Photo: Norbert Schoerner.

Opposite: Two DJs who provided the initial spark for the Acid Jazz scene, Edward Piller and Gilles Peterson, have both gone on to found thriving independent record companies – Acid Jazz Records and Talkin' Loud. The latter's influential group Galliano are pictured *opposite top* in 1992. Acid Jazz's popular *Totally Wired* series (*left*) has featured everything from the Brand New Heavies, Snowboy, D-influence, A Man Called Adam and Mother Earth to rare groove tracks from the 1970s. Cover photo of Totally Wired 6 (*left*): Adam Friedman.

Classic Indie Kid style at the Hackney Homeless Festival in Clissold Park, London, in 1993. Photo: Neil Stevenson.

indie kids cuties grunge & riot grrrls

It was inevitable that the elegant, dressy style of the New Romantics would trigger a response in the opposite direction. It came early in the eighties in Britain with the rise of the Indie Kids – so named because of their allegiance to bands on obscure, independent record labels. Predominantly students, they turned their typically dire financial situation into a proud boast. Their style was (and is) Dressing Down in both senses – anti-elegant and, like the Beats before them, a middle-class (mis?)interpretation of the style of the underprivileged.

The Indie Kids have a comparatively long history and this has given their look time to evolve. Its key ingredients have always been over- or undersized items bought second-hand in charity shops, graphically distinctive T-shirts which indicate interest in some seriously obscure Indie band, battered denim jeans (for girls, often worn cut off with stripy leggings), army surplus garments and big, shiny Dr Marten boots. A variant of this which surfaced later in the eighties was the 'Cutie' look. This too relied heavily on second-hand clothes but concentrated on asexual, pre-adolescent garments and accessories in soft pastel shades. Although the Cutie look was essentially fun and playful, underlying its childlike innocence was a deep-rooted sense of gloom and doom. Indeed, this same pessimism and melancholic introspection is to be found throughout most of the Indie Kid's subculture and is expressed most explicitly in the music of Indie bands such as The Smiths, Joy Division, New Order, Ride, Happy Mondays and My Bloody Valentine.

As the popularity of the British Indie bands grew in the USA, the Indie Kids' appearance style also became influential – especially among students and particularly on the West Coast. In many ways the Seattle-based style which, with much media fanfare, was labelled 'Grunge' in the late eighties can be seen as Indie Kid style with another name. Clearly both looks share the same tattiness, the same reliance on charity or thrift shops, the same love of under/over sizing, the same penchant for checked shirts, the same lank hair and the same chunky workboots. Most fundamentally, like the style of the Indie Kids,

Once purely a Hippy and then a Traveller event, the Glastonbury Festival now attracts followers from an ever-wider range of subcultures. Shown here at the 1993 festival: *far left:* Grunge style (photo: Robbie Crow); *left:* Cutie style (photo: Robbie Crow); *below:* two suitably miserable looking Indie Kids (photo: Jeremy Deller).

Grunge is Dressing Down at its most extreme (with the prosperity of Seattle serving as an appropriate backdrop for a mythologizing of the poor).

Despite these similarities, Grunge should also be considered in its own right and within its own geographic and cultural context. In particular, the Seattle Grunge style of Nirvana, Pearl Jam and Smashing Pumpkins seems to reflect and develop a fusion of Punk and Leftover Hippy aesthetics which is uniquely American. (And which, by the way, is stylistically distinct from the 'Hipunk' fusion exhibited by many British Travellers.)

Historically, going back to the late seventies, while some US Punks took on the full trappings of the British originators (fishnets, stilettos, fetishism, Crazy Colour), the majority interpreted the style more loosely – perhaps drawing upon an older, established American meaning of 'punk' to focus on a general scruffiness which was not all that far removed from the equally unkempt residue left by the Hippies and the counterculture. In this sense Grunge represents no more and no less than the ultimate blend of that wide range of styles (Leftover Hippy, Americanized Punk, Indie Kid) which share a common denominator of Dressing Down.

While on the one hand Grunge has been turned into a meaningless caricature by excessive media attention and high fashion copying, it has also – in response – gone further underground by underlining its Punk roots. This is especially evident in the case of the Riot Grrrls, a network of sassy, assertive young women who have formed a highly articulate, post-feminist subculture first across North America and later into the UK and Europe.

The Riot Grrrls style takes the Punk technique of *bricolage* to its logical conclusion – juxtaposing Cutie-style little-girl dresses with Fredericks of Hollywood tacky glamour, rugged boots, small-town-American second-hand garments, and, especially in the USA, prominent tattoos or piercings. By mixing such apparently opposing styles, the Riot Grrrls are constructing a dialogue on the subject of feminine sexuality and identity which draws as heavily on the unisex practice of the original Punks as it does on feminist theory. Significantly, with the possible exception of the much lampooned boilersuit look of many feminists in the 1970s, the Riot Grrrls have created the first all – or even predominantly – female styletribe in the entire history of streetstyle.

technos & cyberpunks

Cyberpunk style modelled by a member of the Mutoid Waste Company, at a party in King's Cross, London, 1988. Photo: David Swindells.

As 'rave' became a media event and everyone became a 'Raver', a subculture which had given thousands a sense of common identity and purpose dissolved into a fad. It was replaced by many different sub-genres, all aiming to provide a greater specificity. You were into 'progressive house' or 'garage' music and you wore anything from pervy black leather to tongue-in-cheek seventies retro. Anything but a 'Smiley' T-shirt. Any classification except 'Raver'.

The upshot of this variety was a much more exciting, dynamic club culture scene. But it could also be said that that was all it was – lots of clubbers with different musical tastes in an always fluid social whirl which never slowed down long enough to allow new subcultural identities to gell. As I will suggest in the concluding chapter, this post-Rave world typically became a 'Supermarket of Style' in which longterm allegiance to a particular group was superseded by fancy-dress stylistic promiscuity.

But one offshoot of rave culture resists such classification. Instead of 'coming out' into the broader, more diffuse club scene, the Technos chose instead to go further and further into the synthetic, rapidly beating heart of acid house. In their journey through rave and its immediate antecedents the Technos found themselves in the company of early electronic experimenters like Kraftwerk and Tangerine Dream. From this pre-rave point they blasted off into a post-rave world whose intense and uncompromising stance effectively excluded the trendy and faint-hearted.

Like their ear-splitting, mechanical music, their clothing styles resisted fashionable imitation. Dressed in anti-radiation suits and

masks, flak jackets and urban commando camouflage, the Technos looked like something out of a sci-fi disaster movie. Hard and foreboding, their SAS-like image perfectly matched their 'difficult' music. Despite or because of this, by the early nineties they had become an enormous subculture stretching from Berlin to Tokyo.

Trendy London typically saw them as a bit of a joke. Their roots were in the more obscure suburbs and in small, out-of-the-way towns to which the media rarely ventured. Furthermore, here at last was a subculture which was focused neither in Britain nor in the USA. To get to the heart of Techno you had to go to Berlin, Frankfurt or Ghent. (Ghent? Yes, it's in Belgium. Belgium? Yes, and this has nothing to do with the Eurovision Song Contest.)

With a long history of electronic music experimentation and an industrial imagery as old as *Metropolis*, Northern Europe is the obvious habitat for Techno. And so is Japan, where technology-crazy young people known as 'Otaku' have made it a way of life.

In their delight in technology and their futuristic vision the Technos are determinedly out of step with that search for a cosy, mythic past which so often typifies our nostalgia-obsessed age. Their natural compatriots are the Cyberpunks, who for more than a decade have been using computer networks and the promise of virtual reality to bring the present into the future. Where the latter group differs from the former, however, as its name suggests, is in its punkish radicalism.

While the Technos seem focused only on the objective of technologically enhanced leisure pursuits, the Cyberpunks are determined to use technological advances to effect change in all aspects of society. As well as embracing everything from virtual reality sex to holographic fabrics, they also propose an undermining of hierarchical authority structures by means of accessible computer networks and freeform information channels.

Although their language and imagery are far removed from 'the spirit of '76', the Cyberpunks' vision is fully in tune with that of the original Punks, who (as in Derek Jarman's film *Jubilee*) saw the future in terms

**Techno musician Richard James – The Aphex Twin – London, 1993.
Photo: Wolfgang Tillmans.**

Cyberpunk style, as worn by (*clockwise from left*) Romanian-Italian clothing and jewelry designer Crudelia Demon, English lorry driver Robin Brown and Australian 'international nomad' Donna Nolan. Photos: Steve Pyke. Styled by Gavin Fernandes, 1991.

of societal collapse and endemic tribalism. What the Cyberpunks propose is simply that each of these isolated tribes link together via post-industrial technology to create an alternative, non-hierarchical structure.

Unlike the Punks, the Cyberpunks have not generally relied on a distinctive appearance style to proclaim their subcultural identity. The movement began more than a decade ago as a science-fiction-influenced literary genre and its exponents (beyond a liking for mirror-coated sunglasses) just looked like scruffy computer boffins.

But in the early nineties, especially on the streets of London and in clubs like Torture Garden and Submission, which delight in an exciting blend of Techno and Pervy Futurist styles, one can see the beginnings of a new breed of Cyberpunk. They look like a cross between *Mad Max* and *Blade Runner*. Using the same *bricolage* techniques pioneered by the Punks, they juxtapose 'found' industrial waste (hubcaps, gasmasks, rubber tubing) with state-of-the-art technology and holographic fabrics.

With an image as inventive and radical as their ideology, this new breed of Cyberpunks offers a powerful vision of the twenty-first century and demonstrates that – fifty years on from the Zooties – street and club style still has the ability to surprise and even to shock.

the gathering of the tribes

Top: Jean, Traveller and tepee dweller, at the Forest Fayre, Forest of Dean, Gloucestershire, 1991. Photo: Alan Lodge.

Above: Very Ambient DJ MixMaster Morris in holographic jacket by Space Time, Brixton, London, 1993. Photo: Robbie Crow.

Left: Spiky Latex outfit designed by Craig Morrison on display at the Cyberseed Night at the Fridge, Brixton, London, 1993. Photo: Neil Stevenson.

The history of streetstyle is one of ever-increasing variety and personal choice. Back in the 1940s a young black man living in Harlem could choose between conventional attire and the zoot suit. In the same era a young white male in, say, Texas could step out in an embroidered Western-Style shirt and a stetson. But in both cases choice was limited to an either/or proposition – 'normal' dress versus one particular form of streetstyle.

Multiple-choice options did not actually appear until the sixties (in Britain, for example, there were Mods *or* Rockers) but even then the evidence shows that an individual's socio-economic background often limited such choice (with Rockers tending to come from the working class and Mods from lower-middle-class backgrounds). It was only after Punk in the late seventies that a rapid escalation in the number of styletribes left young people with a real range of options. These increased dramatically only a few years later in the wake of the New Romantics and there was a similar fragmentation of youth culture in the late eighties, when the rave scene splintered apart. The result was that by the start of the nineties streetstyle was characterized by an extraordinary heterogeneity. Hardcore Ravers, Technos, Cyberpunks, Travellers, Indie Kids, Skaters, B-Boys/Flygirls, Goths, Pervs, Grungies, Acid Jazzers, Raggamuffins and so on were all viable subcultural options.

This diversity was accompanied by fusions between various existing groups. As we have seen, even remarkably dissimilar subcultures like the Ravers and the Travellers began to overlook their differences in the late eighties as they explored common concerns and problems. As more and more diverse groups joined in this spirit of mutual respect the nineties saw the beginnings of a remarkable 'Gathering of the Tribes'. Suddenly the synthesized sounds of Techno could be heard at once-purist Travellers' festivals, and clubs opened which were characterized by a 'come one come all' ecumenism.

For example, in London's Megadog and Megatripolis clubs an ever more catholic mix

Above left: British environmental protest group, The Donga Tribe, 1993. Photo: Zed Nelson.
Above right: Guests at the Megatripolis Club, London, 1993. Photo: David Swindells.

of both music and appearance styles made it hard to know whether you were at a Techno rave or a Hippy love-in. And the same was true outside London at illegal festivals/raves put on by 'sound system' renegades like Spiral Tribe, who sought with great determination to join all strands of contemporary alternative culture.

Anthropologists noted long ago that the traditional tribes of the Third World put aside their factional differences when faced by a larger, outside threat. Clearly something similar is going on among the styletribes of our own world. But what is the larger, outside force which is having this harmonizing effect?

Though the heavy-handedness of the police in shutting down both raves and festivals is perhaps the most obvious candidate, there are other factors that should be considered. In particular, excessive media attention has often had the effect of undermining subcultural integrity, as has fashion's increasing tendency instantly to convert streetstyle into the latest trend. Today, members of all styletribes are acutely aware of this dual threat and this awareness has become part of the common ground between diverse subcultures.

In effect, as fashion and the media have conspired to blur the boundaries between 'them' and 'us', the realization has grown that the most significant line to be drawn in the sand is the one between those who have a genuine commitment to *any and all* subcultural groups and those who simply treat such styletribes as an amusing joke and/or an inspiration for the latest fashion.

In light of this realization even the stylistic and ideological differences separating, for example, the Technos and the Travellers pale into insignificance and a common enemy is identified: all those who play at being 'street' but who are unwilling to make a serious commitment to a particular subculture. In this sense the Gathering of the Tribes represents the only appropriate response to our mainstream culture's ever growing fascination with streetstyle and youthculture. (Which this book, of course, both reflects and promotes.)

Whatever the cause, today's Gathering of the Tribes has also had a profound effect within these subcultures themselves. Most intriguingly, it has had the effect of producing more rather than fewer styletribe options.

For me, a useful (if obscure) analogy can be made with those huge experiments in physics which are currently being conducted in places like the C.E.R.N. facilities in Switzerland. As diverse, unlikely atoms are brought together they give off a host of tiny, often bizarre, sub-atomic particles. In a similar way, in 'experimental research facilities' like Megadog and Megatripolis, and at Spiral Tribe events, where radically different subcultures like the Travellers and the Ravers come into contact, the result is an exploding galaxy of tiny, sub-atomic *microtribes*. A few of these, such as the Ambient Technos, the Zippies and the Donga Tribe, are just about discernible to the outside observer, but most are not. But despite such confusion (itself a logical, defensive objective of all tribalists today) it is nevertheless clear that all manner of extraordinary hybrids are in the process of evolving.

Also apparent is the way in which such 'narrow-casting' of subcultural identities is exponentially increasing yet again the number and range of available options. Instead of homogeneous amalgamation into one mega-subculture, the Gathering of the Tribes has simply served to create a huge umbrella under which all sorts of previously untenable experiments can be conducted. Aside from its potential for the creation of an astounding number of new subcultures, what is truly remarkable about this situation is the non-hierarchical way in which all these groups relate to each other – with no one claiming a monopoly of wisdom and all open to further cross-fertilization. Here is the Hippies' New Age, the Punks' Tribalism and the Technos' and Cyberpunks' post-industrial vision all rolled into one. At Megadog one sees the future . . . and it works.

the supermarket of style

Above: Musician and style test pilot Johnny Slut with a literal interpretation of the Supermarket of Style, photographed by the author in the London Underground, late 1980s.

Right: Japanese teenager 'YoYo' photographed in her own clothes by Yasuhide Kuge for *Cutie* magazine, 1992.

Apart from its astounding variety, streetstyle today is characterized by the extent to which it exists within the shadow of its own past. In one sense this state of affairs simply reflects the obvious fact that it now *has* a past – with some five decades stacked on top of each other. But at the same time the significance of this history has been magnified by the extent to which popular culture – and with it, of course, youthculture and streetstyle – has moved further and further centre stage as a defining feature of 'Western Society'.

This fact of late-twentieth-century life is especially noticeable in its effect upon the present generation of youth. Reared on a constant diet of television programmes and magazine articles about previous decades and Jurassic styletribes, they are *knowing* in a way that previous generations were not.

Many who weren't even born in 1976 know all about Punk as if it had happened yesterday and they too had been pogoing down at the Vortex. Nor is this the limit of their knowledge: Glam, the Hippies, Swinging London, the Mods and Rockers, the original Rockabillies (as well as their eighties reincarnation as 'Cats') and even the Teddy Boys are all part of their pop culture education.

The effects of this can be readily seen in contemporary pop videos, where caricatured figures from the entire history of streetstyle flash before the eyes in the course of three minutes. While my own generation (the 'baby boomers') looked back, if at all, in anger, the present generation seems sometimes to be so engulfed by the past that it is hard to discern their present, let alone their future.

Needless to say, this tendency towards nostalgia is having its own effect upon contemporary streetstyle. While five decades of rebellious teenagers explicitly set out to create new styletribes which (at least in their mythology) kicked aside their parents' past, since at least the mid-eighties we have been witness to a seemingly never-ending proliferation of Neo-Mods, Neo-Teds, Neo-Hippies, Neo-Psychedelics, Neo-Punks and now even Neo-New Romantics.

Usually obsessed with historical accuracy, the young members of these various retro-groups are determined to recreate the look and the spirit of their respective subculture's golden age – pointedly discounting the effect of years of inaccurate media stereotyping in the process. In this way the young members of contemporary groups like The Edwardian Drape Society (T.E.D.S.) are keeping alive a subculture which might have faded into absurd caricature when its zimmer-frame-pushing original members finally hung up their drapes for the last time.

A rather different approach to a present reality which is so rooted in the past is what I call 'The Supermarket of Style'. Here, instead of focusing upon a particular styletribe of yesteryear, all of history's streetstyles, from Zooties to Beatniks, Hippies to Punks, are lined up as possible options as if they were cans of soup on supermarket shelves.

While retro-groups like the T.E.D.S. exhibit a commitment to their chosen group which is, if anything, even more devout than that of its original members, those who frequent the Supermarket of Style display instead a stylistic promiscuity which is breathtaking in its casualness. 'Punks' one day, 'Hippies' the next, they fleetingly leap across decades and ideological divides – converting the history of streetstyle into a vast themepark.

All of which fits very neatly within postmodern theory. In Style World, 'nostalgia mode' is set at full tilt, separate eras are flung together in one stretched, 'synchronic' moment in time, all reality is hype and 'authenticity' seems out of the question. This is not, however, a world devoid of meaning. Indeed, precisely the opposite. Those who shop at the Supermarket of Style know full well that every garment (a 'target' T-shirt or one with Queen Elizabeth II sporting a safety pin through her nose) and every accessory on offer (Hippy beads, Psychedelic plastic rings) comes as part of a complete semiological package deal.

But by jumping around and through history – by discarding one subcultural package on the floor as they pick up another

Running parallel to Carnaby Street, Newburgh Street in West Soho, London, has arguably been more important in terms of stylistic influence. This 1993 photograph by the author mimics the 1967 display of Newburgh Street style which appears on page 62 and features designs by (*left to right*) Jacqueline Hancher, Pam Hogg, Bond, John Richmond and Helen Storey.

In London the Supermarket of Style spirit is epitomized by the Sign of the Times shops and theme party events. Shown here, *clockwise from top left*, 1950s-inspired baby-doll nightie and other looks for 1994. Two revellers at 'Shampoo Planet' event, 1993. A clubber in a dress made from wooden car seat covers at 'Top of the Pops' event, 1992. Matching clubbers for 'Night Boat to Cairo' event, 1993. Postmodern 'Punk': top designed by 'Joie' and Union Jack trousers by Jimmy Jumble from Sign of the Times, 1993. All photos: Jeremy Deller. Styling *top left*: Sidonie Barton.

– the clubbers who shop in the Supermarket of Style and who live and play in Style World thumb their noses at the very history which weighs so heavily upon their generation. They seem to be saying, 'Yes, sure, we know about Mods, Punks, Hippies and Psychedelics. It's our cultural heritage, for heaven's sake. But we've got our own lives to lead and so we take it all with a healthy pinch of salt.'

Although the Supermarket of Style has been a long time in the making, its existence became obvious at that moment late in the eighties when the Ravers collapsed as a singular, coherent subculture. As the younger members of this group circled in upon themselves to form tighter, more precisely bounded styletribes like the Technos, another, larger and mainly older group drifted into a more fluid, trendier club scene. Doggedly determined to break free of the label 'Ravers', they typically at the same time stepped beyond all subcultural classification and entered instead a quick-change Style World where no one 'uniform' would become a straightjacket.

In the process they created a sort of laboratory in which to experiment with all those streetstyle looks which had been

Arguably, the Supermarket of Style approach to dress first emerged in Japan, where fifty years of Western streetstyle and at least fifty different Western subcultures have long been both an obsession and a source of inspiration. Shown here, *clockwise from top left*, Shin and Kimiko – designers for Beauty & Beast fashion company in Osaka, 1994.
Photo: Adam Howe.
Three Japanese teenage boys photographed in their own clothes by Yasuhide Kuge for *Cutie* magazine, 1992.
Pop/house music group More Deep performing in Tokyo, 1992.
Photo: Mark Wigan.
Sampling and mixing workwear, Hippy and Biker styles, Tokyo, 1992. Photo: Norbert Schoerner.
Sexy 'Body Con' style flaunted outside Club Juliana's in Tokyo, 1992. Photo: Norbert Schoerner.

Supermarket of Style looks displayed in Club Yellow, Tokyo, 1992.
Photos: Norbert Schoerner and Adam Howe.

'Fetish fashion'-inspired clubbers outside Picasso's (later Club Yellow), Tokyo, 1992. Photo: Adam Howe.

accumulating over some fifty years – reprocessing them with a delightful sense of irony, deconstructing the old into something new. What the Supermarket of Style is not, however, is a subculture which provides a sense of belonging in return for a lifelong stylistic and ideological commitment. This is not, in other words, the Bracknell Chopper Club, where a tattooed insignia marks membership 'forever'.

Nor, therefore, are the denizens of the Supermarket of Style comparable to the Teds, the Beats, the Mods, the Rockers, the Hippies, the Skinheads, the Headbangers, the Punks or the Goths. And, in this sense, neither are they comparable to all those Travellers, Zippies, Ambient Technos, Hardcore Ravers, Dongas and so forth whose Gathering of the Tribes we considered earlier.

The Supermarket of Style is much too fast-changing and loosely structured to qualify as a 'tribe' in any true sense of the term. This is not, however, to brand those

within it as just a bunch of good-time party-goers. They are this to be sure, but underneath all the fancy dress and the posturing there is an attempt to construct a new visual language which will make it possible to say something fresh in an age when we've heard it all before.

At its most effective and startling, this language reduces whole subcultures from the history of streetstyle to simple 'adjectives' – Hippy beads, Skinhead/Punk DMs, Mod target motifs, Rocker leather, Perv rubber, Glam sequins – and juxtaposes these in a single outfit. As in contemporary pop music, this might be termed 'sampling & mixing' – taking little snatches ('samples') from the past and mixing them together.

If earlier I likened the Supermarket of Style to a shop where various streetstyles are on offer as if they were cans of different kinds of soup, here we are talking about opening all the cans up and throwing a spoonful from each into one pot. Or perhaps just a selection

carefully calculated to shock the palate. For, let us not forget, this generation not only knows what different streetstyles look like, they are fully aware of the subcultural meanings which each 'uniform' was designed to convey. What is being sampled & mixed, therefore, are ideological as well as aesthetic differences. To combine Hippy naturalness with Pervy plastic is to play with meaning as well as with style.

In the end, such experiments in the Supermarket of Style are coming up with the same sort of results as those produced within the Gathering of the Tribes: new, unexpected possibilities born of unlikely partners. Streetstyle is not what it used to be – we are all too sophisticated to relive those days when standing around on a streetcorner in a leather jacket was a simple, exuberant act of rebellion – but it is still a remarkably illuminating reflection of the times and a succinct, powerful and alluring vision of the alternative.

BLOW UP

DAZED &CONFUSED™

1 DAVE @ LOVE RANCH • 2 PRINCE @ GLAM • 3 YVETTE @ LOVE RANCH • 4 JACKI @ CLAM • 5 MATTHEW @ SMASHING • 6 SONY @ MINISTRY • 7 SQUIRREL @ JERRY • 8 CLAM • 9 NYOMI @ GOOD ENOUGH • 10 STEWART @ MINISTRY • 11 STEPHANIE @ GOOD ENOUGH • 12 DESERT @ MINISTRY • 13 BELSTELL WORK @ LOVE RANCH • 14 BEN @ SMALL'S • 15 JAMAL @ FANTASTIC • 16 CAPTAIN @ KINKY DISCO • 17 WYNN @ GOOD ENOUGH • 18 JACQUI @ LOVE RANCH • 19 FIZZY @ FANTASTIC • 20 MARTIN (OR GERRY) @ CAO BABY • 21 THOMAS @ SMASHING • 22 A GIRL @ LOVE RANCH • 23 LOUISE @ LOVE RANCH • 24 FRANCESCA @ GLAM • 25 JOEY @ SMASHING

APOLOGIES FOR ANY WRONG OR ABSENT NAMES... WE COULDN'T READ YOUR WRITING! WITH THANKS TO NICK @ PHOTOFUSION

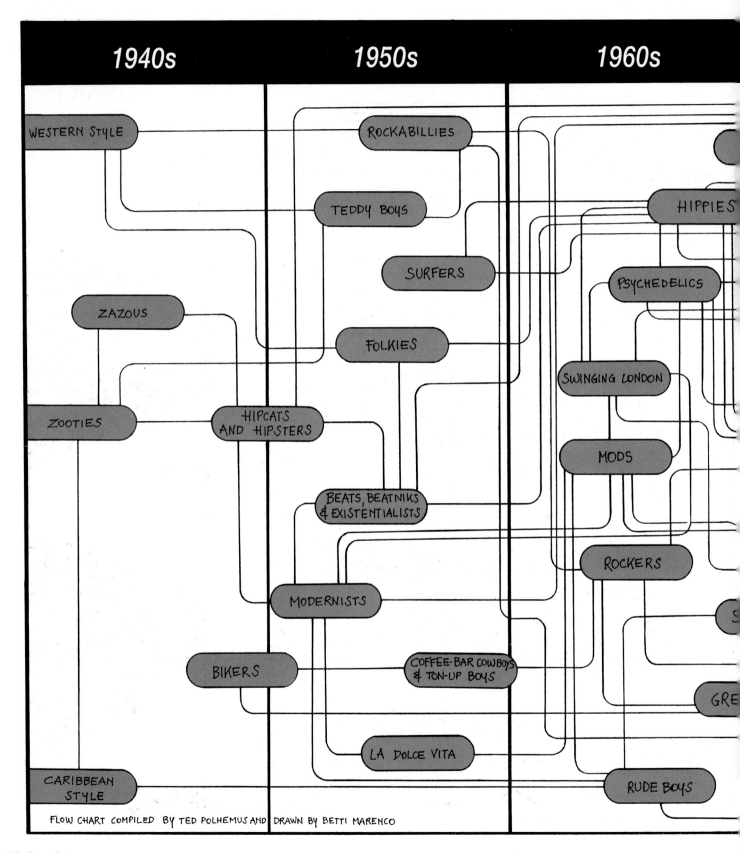

WESTERN STYLE

ROCKABILLIES

TEDDY BOYS

SURFERS

ZAZOUS

FOLKIES

HIPPIES

PSYCHEDELICS

SWINGING LONDON

ZOOTIES

HIPCATS AND HIPSTERS

MODS

BEATS, BEATNIKS & EXISTENTIALISTS

ROCKERS

MODERNISTS

BIKERS

COFFEE-BAR COWBOYS & TON-UP BOYS

GRE

LA DOLCE VITA

CARIBBEAN STYLE

RUDE BOYS

FLOW CHART COMPILED BY TED POLHEMUS AND DRAWN BY BETTI MARENCO

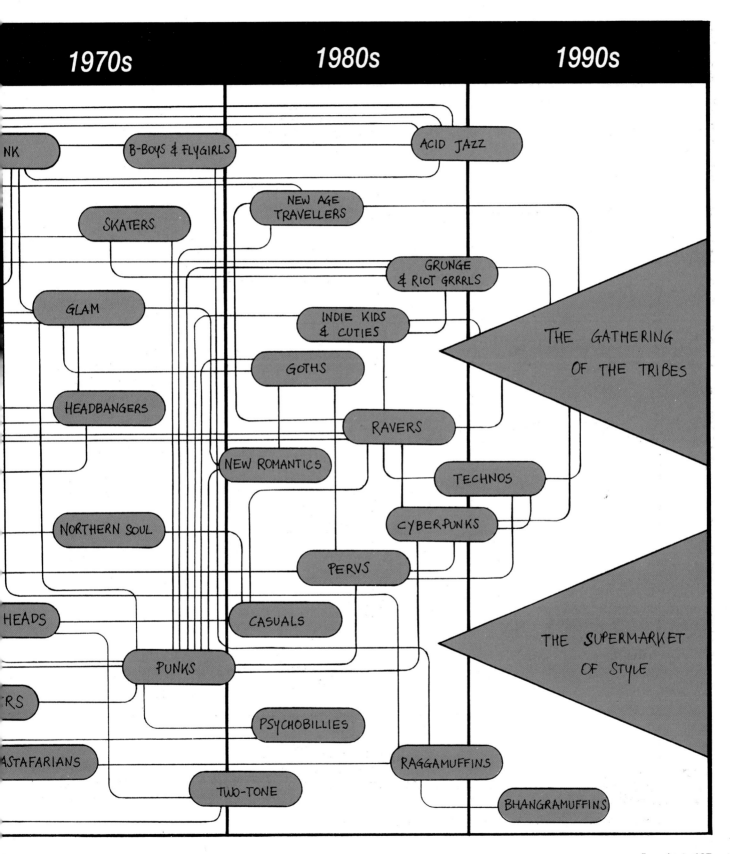

notes

trickle down/bubble up
1 Peter York, *Modern Times*, London, 1994, p. 10.
2 Mick Farren, *The Black Leather Jacket*, London, 1985.
3 In conversation with the author, 1994.
4 Speaking on 'Reportage', BBC 2, 26 January 1994.

zooties
1 Malcolm X (with Alex Haley), *The Autobiography of Malcolm X*, London, 1968, p. 135.
2 J. C. Flügel, *The Psychology of Clothes*, London, 1971, pp. 110–119.
3 *Ibid*.
4 *The New Yorker*, 1941.
5 Stuart Cosgrove, 'The Zoot Suit and Style Warfare: An Anthology of Fashion and Music', in Angela McRobbie, ed., *Zoot Suits and Second-hand Dresses*, London, 1989, p. 4.
6 Malcolm X (with Alex Haley), *The Autobiography of Malcolm X*, London, 1968, p. 164.

zazous
1 Farid Chenoune, *A History of Men's Fashion*, Paris, 1993, p. 210.

western style
1 Patrick Carr, 'The Changing Image of Country Music', in the Country Music Foundation, eds, *Country: The Music and the Musicians*, New York, 1988, p. 496.
2 *Ibid*.
3 Jo Anne Olian, ed., *Everyday Fashions of the Forties: As Pictured in Sears Catalogs*, New York, 1992, pp. 81, 92, 93.

bikers
1 Mick Farren, *The Black Leather Jacket*, London, 1985, p. 39.
2 *Ibid*., p. 38.

hip cats & hipsters
1 Mick Farren, *The Black Leather Jacket*, London, 1985.

beats, beatniks & existentialists
1 Jack Kerouac, *On the Road*, London, 1991, p. 159.
2 In particular, Herb Caen writing in the *San Francisco Chronicle* in 1957, the 'nik' alluding to the 'Sputnik' satellite, thereby identifying the Beats with communism.

teddy boys
1 Jon Savage, 'Teds', *The Face* 26 (June 1982): 12–15.

modernists
1 Joe Goldberg, 'The Birth of Cool', in Gene Sculatti, ed., *A Catalog of Cool*, New York, 1982, p. 4.
2 *Ibid*., p. 5.
3 Richard Williams, *Miles Davis: The Man in the Green Shirt*, London, 1993 (extract in *Independent on Sunday Magazine* (24 October 1993): 29).
4 Joe Goldberg, 'The Birth of Cool', in Gene Sculatti, ed., *A Catalog of Cool*, New York, 1982, p. 4.

coffee-bar cowboys & ton-up boys
1 Johnny Stuart, *Rockers!*, London, 1987, pp. 17–18.

surfers
1 Tom Wolfe, *The Pump House Gang*, London, 1992, pp. 13–30.

mods
1 Colin MacInnes, *Absolute Beginners*, London, 1992, p. 62.
2 *Ibid*., p. 63.
3 Nik Cohn, 'Today There Are No Gentlemen', in *Ball the Wall*, London, 1989, p. 29.

rockers
1 Johnny Stuart, *Rockers!*, London, 1987, p. 88.

rude boys & two-tone
1 Carol Tulloch, 'Rebel without a Pause: Black Streetstyle & Black Designers', in Julia Ash and Elizabeth Wilson, eds, *Chic Thrills*, London, 1992, p. 87.
2 *Ibid*.
3 Dick Hebdige, 'Reggae, Rastas and Rudies; Style and the Subversion of Form', Stencilled Paper 24, Centre for Contemporary Culture Studies, University of Birmingham, 1974, p. 26.

greasers
1 Johnny Stuart, *Rockers!*, London, 1987.

skinheads
1 Nick Knight, *Skinheads*, London, 1982, p. 23.
2 Quoted in George Marshall, *Spirit of '69: A Skinhead Bible*, Dunoon, Scotland, 1991, p. 139.

funk
1 Tom Wolfe, 'Funky Chic', in *Mauve Gloves & Madmen, Clutter & Vine*, New York, 1977, pp. 183–84.
2 *Ibid*., p. 188.

headbangers
1 Iain Chambers, *Urban Rhythms: Pop Music and Popular Culture*, London, 1985, p. 123.

new romantics
1 From the film *Young Soul Rebels*, directed by Isaac Julien (GB 1991).

casuals
1 Kevin Sampson, 'The Ins and Outs of High Street Fashion', *The Face* 39 (July 1983): 22–25.

raggamuffins
1 Dick Hebdige, *Cut 'N' Mix: Culture, Identity and Caribbean Music*, London, 1987, pp. 123–24.

further information

hanging out
selected reading
Baudrillard, Jean, *Revenge of the Crystal*, London, 1990.
Chambers, Iain, *Border Dialogues: Journeys in Postmodernity*, London, 1990.
Jameson, Frederic, *Postmodernism or the Cultural Logic of Late Capitalism*, London, 1991.

trickle down/bubble up
selected reading
Farren, Mick, *The Black Leather Jacket*, London, 1985.
Polhemus, Ted, and Procter, Lynn, *Fashion & Anti-Fashion*, London, 1978.
—, *Pop Styles*, London, 1984.
Polhemus, Ted, *Bodystyles*, Luton, Beds., 1988.
York, Peter, *Modern Times*, London, 1984.

tribal styles
selected reading
Polhemus, Ted (ed.), *Social Aspects of the Human Body*, London, 1978.
magazines
Body Art, Publications Ltd., PO Box 32, Great Yarmouth, Norfolk NR29 5RD

zooties
selected reading
Carr, Roy, Case, Brian, and Dellar, Fred, *The Hip: Hipsters, Jazz and the Beat Generation*, London, 1986.
Cosgrove, Stuart, 'The Zoot Suit and Style Warfare: An Anthology of Fashion and Music', in Angela McRobbie, ed., *Zoot Suits and Second-hand Dresses*, London, 1989.
Elms, Robert, 'Rise of the Young Turk', *The Face* 20 (December 1981): 8–12.
Malcolm X (with Alex Haley), *The Autobiography of Malcolm X*, New York, 1965.
Sullivan, Chris, 'The Zoot Suit – A Historical Perspective', *The Face* 17 (September 1981): 50–51.
music
Calloway, Cab, *Minnie The Moocher* (1933)
Ellington, Duke, *Take The 'A' Train* (1940)
Gaillard, Slim, *Dunkin' Bagel* (1939)
Jefferson, Eddie, *There I Go, There I Go Again* (1941)
Young, Lester, *Jumpin' With Symphony Sid* (1942)
films
Cabin in the Sky, Vincente Minnelli (US 1943)
Stormy Weather, Andrew Stone (US 1943)
Malcolm X, Spike Lee (US 1992)

zazous
selected reading
Bollon, Patrice, *Morale du Masque*, Paris, 1990.
Chenoune, Farid, *A History of Men's Fashion*, Paris, 1993.
Loiseau, Jean-Claude, *Les Zazous*, Paris, 1977.
music
Calloway, Cab, *Zaz Zuh Zaz* (1939)

Hess, Johnny, *Je Suis Swing* (1939)
Hess, Johnny, *Ils Sont Zazous* (1942)
Trenet, Charles, *Poule Zazou* (n.d.)
films
Hollywood Hotel, Busby Berkeley (US 1937)
Mademoiselle Swing, Richard Pottier (France 1942)

caribbean style
selected reading
Hijuelos Oscar, *Mambo Kings Play Songs of Love*, New York and London, 1989.
'Fiesta! Latino', *i-D* 62 (September 1988): entire issue.
Tulloch, Carol, 'Rebel without a Pause: Black Streetstyle & Black Designers', in Julia Ash and Elizabeth Wilson, eds, *Chic Thrills*, London, 1992.

western style
selected reading
Birch, Ian, 'The Original Rhinestoned Cowboy', *The Face* 30 (October 1982): 52–55.
The Country Music Foundation, eds, *Country: The Music and the Musicians*, New York, 1988.
Finlayson, Iain, *Denim*, Norwich, 1990.
Graveline, Noel, *Jeans: Levi's Story*, Geneva-Paris, 1990.
Malone, Bill C., *Country Music U.S.A.*, Austin, Texas, 1991.
music
Cash, Johnny, *Folsom Prison Blues* (1956)
Cline, Patsy, *Walkin' After Midnight* (1960)
Jones, George, *The Race Is On* (1955)
Williams, Hank, *Your Cheatin' Heart* (1952)
Yoakam, Dwight, *Guitars, Cadillacs* (1984)
films
Your Cheatin' Heart, Gene Nelson (US 1964)
Nashville, Robert Altman (US 1975)
A Coal Miner's Daughter, Michael Apted (US 1980)
Urban Cowboy, James Bridges (US 1980)
Tender Mercies, Bruce Beresford (US 1982)
Sweet Dreams, Karel Reisz (US 1985)
Thing Called Love, Peter Bogdanovich (US 1993)
magazines
Lonesome No More (see below)
organizations
The Country Music Association, Suite 3, 52 Haymarket, London SW1 4RP; tel: 071 930 2445
The Country Music Federation, 1 Music Circle South, Nashville, TN 37203, USA
Lonesome No More, 112c Agar Grove, London NW1 9TY; tel: 071 485 2547

bikers
selected reading
Briggs, Victor, ed., *The World of Hells Angels*, London, 1972.
Farren, Mick, *The Black Leather Jacket*, London, 1985.
Harris, Maz, *Bikers*, London, 1985.
Kershaw, Andy, 'Hell's Archangel', *Observer Magazine* (19 September 1993): 12–19.
Stuart, Johnny, *Rockers!*, London, 1987.

films

The Wild One, Laslo Benedek (US 1954)
Motorcycle Gang, Edward L. Cahn (US 1957)
Dragstrip Riot, David Bradley (US 1958)
The Loveless, Kathryn Bigelow (US 1983)

hip cats & hipsters

selected reading

Bergerot, Frank, and Merlin, Arnaud, *The Story of Jazz: Bop and Beyond*, London, 1993.
Carr, Roy, Case, Brian, and Dellar, Fred, *The Hip: Hipsters, Jazz and the Beat Generation*, London, 1986.
Davis, Miles (with Quincy Troupe), *Miles: The Autobiography*, New York, 1989.
Gottlieb, William P., *The Golden Age of Jazz*, New York, 1993.
Hebdige, Dick, *Subculture: The Meaning of Style*, London, 1979.
Thorne, Tony, *Fads, Fashions & Cults: From Acid House to Zoot Suit*, London, 1993.

music

Blakey, Art, *Cubano Chant* (n.d.)
Parker, Charlie, and Gillespie, Dizzy, *A Night In Tunisia* (1951)
Rollins, Sonny, *Mambo Bounce* (1948)
Silver, Horace, and Blakey, Art, *Quick Silver* (1956)
Young, Lester, *Lester Leaps In* (1949)

films

Bird, Clint Eastwood (US 1988)

magazines

Straight No Chaser, 41 Coronet Street, London N1 6HD

beats, beatniks & existentialists

selected reading

Carr, Roy, Case, Brian, and Dellar, Fred, *The Hip: Hipsters, Jazz and the Beat Generation*, London, 1986.
Cassady, Carolyn, *Off the Road: 20 Years with Cassady, Kerouac and Ginsberg*, London, 1991.
Davis, Miles (with Quincy Troupe), *Miles: The Autobiography*, New York, 1989.
Ginsberg, Allen, *Howl*, San Francisco, 1956.
Kerouac, Jack, *On the Road*, New York, 1957.
—, *The Subterraneans*, New York, 1958.

films

Expresso Bongo, Val Guest (GB 1959)
Pull My Daisy, Robert Frank (US 1959)
The Subterraneans, Ranald MacDougall (US 1960)
Naked Lunch, David Cronenberg (Canada/GB 1991)

magazines

The Beat Scene, Kevin Ring (ed.), 27 Court Leet, Binleywoods, Coventry CV3 2JQ
Kerouac Connection, Mitchel Smith (ed.), PO Box 462004, Escondido, CA 92046–2004, USA

teddy boys

selected reading

Chenoune, Farid, *A History of Men's Fashion*, Paris, 1993.
Cohn, Nik, 'Today There Are No Gentlemen', in *Ball the Wall*, London, 1989.

Hebdige, Dick, *Subculture: The Meaning of Style*, London, 1979.
Ingledew, Jon, 'Barry Island/Butlins 24–27.9.83', *i-D* 14 (July 1984): 50–51.
Lewis, Peter, *The 50s*, London, 1978.
Pearce, Christopher, *Fifties Source Book*, London, 1990.
Powell, Polly, and Peel, Lucy, *'50s & '60s Style*, London, 1988.
Savage, Jon, 'Teds', *The Face* 26 (June 1982): 12–15.
Steele-Perkins, Chris, and Smith, Richard, *The Teds*, London, 1979.

music

The Cadillacs, *Gloria* (1954)
Cochran, Eddie, *C'mon Everybody* (1959)
Bill Haley & the Comets, *Rock Around The Clock (1955)*
Little Richard, *Tutti Frutti* (1957)
Self, Ronnie, *Bop-A-Lena* (1958)

films

Violent Playground, James Kennaway (GB 1958)
The Boys, Sidney J. Furie (GB 1962)

magazines

Rumble, c/o 22 Creighton Road, London NW6 6ED

organizations

The Edwardian Drape Society (T.E.D.S.), 15 Denbigh Street, London SW1V 2HF

modernists

selected reading

Davis, Miles (with Quincy Troupe), *Miles: The Autobiography*, New York, 1989.
Fordham, John, *The Sound of Jazz*, New York, 1989.
Goldberg, Joe, 'The Birth of Cool', in Gene Sculatti, ed., *A Catalog of Cool*, New York, 1982.
Gottlieb, William P., *The Golden Age of Jazz*, New York, 1993.
Williams, Richard, *Miles Davis: The Man in the Green Shirt*, London, 1993.

music

Dave Brubeck Quartet, *Take Five* (1961)
Coltrane, John, *A Love Supreme* (1965)
Davis, Miles, *Kind Of Blue* (1959)
Modern Jazz Quartet, *The Jasmin Tree* (1982)
Morgan, Lee, *The Sidewinder* (1962)

films

Let's Get Lost, Bruce Weber (US 1989)
Malcolm X, Spike Lee (US 1992)

magazines

Straight No Chaser, 41 Coronet Street, London N1 6HD

folkies

selected reading

Melly, George, *Revolt into Style*, Oxford, 1989.
Tarrant, Chris, *Rebel Rebel: 25 Years of Teenage Trauma*, London, 1991.

music

Ives, Burl, *Top Of Old Smokey* (n.d.)
Murphy, Delia, *Spinning Wheel* (n.d.)
Shand, Jimmy, *Bluebell Polka* (1955)
The Weavers, *Wimoweh* (1952)
White, Josh, *Saint James Infirmary* (n.d.)

films

The Grapes of Wrath, John Ford (US 1940)

magazines

Folk Roots, PO Box 337, London N4 1TW

rockabillies

selected reading

Jones, Dylan, *Haircuts*, London, 1990.
Malone, Bill C., *Country Music U.S.A.*, Austin, Texas, 1991.
Palmer, Robert, 'Get Rhythm: Elvis Presley, Johnny Cash, and the Rockabillies', in the Country Music Foundation, eds, *Country: The Music and the Musicians*, New York, 1988.

music

Bennett, Boyd, *My Boy Flat-top* (1958)
Burnette, Johnny, *Lonesome Train* (1956)
MacCurtis, *If I Had Me A Woman* (n.d.)
Orbison, Roy, *Domino* (1956)
Presley, Elvis, *That's Alright* (1954)

films

Rebel without a Cause, Nicholas Ray (US 1955)
Hot Rod Gang, Lew Landers (US 1958)
King Creole, Michael Curtiz (US 1958)

la dolce vita

selected reading

Chenoune, Farid, *A History of Men's Fashion*, Paris, 1993.
Cohn, Nik, 'Today There Are No Gentlemen', in *Ball the Wall*, London, 1989.
Powell, Polly, and Peel, Lucy, *'50s & '60s Style*, London, 1988.

films

I Vitelloni, Federico Fellini (Italy/France 1953)
Roman Holiday, William Wyler (US 1953)
La Dolce Vita, Federico Fellini (Italy/France 1960)

coffee-bar cowboys & ton-up boys

selected reading

Clay, Mike, *Café Racers: Rockers, Rock 'N' Roll and the Coffee-Bar Cult*, London, 1988.
Farren, Mick, *The Black Leather Jacket*, London, 1985.
Stuart, Johnny, *Rockers!*, London, 1987.

films

The Damned, Joseph Losey (GB 1961)
Some People, Clive Donner (GB 1962)
The Leather Boys, Sidney J. Furie (GB 1963)

surfers

selected reading

Beard, Steve, 'Waves of Glory', *Arena* (1993): 92–99.
Hoffman, Flippy, 'The Wild Frontier', *Surfing* (May 1992): 40–43.
Steele, H. Thomas, *The Hawaiian Shirt*, London, 1984.
Wolfe, Tom, *The Pump House Gang*, New York, 1968, 1992.
Young, Nat, *The History of Surfing*, Tucson, Ariz., 1987.

films

Gidget, Paul Wendkos (US 1959)
The Endless Summer, Bruce Brown (US 1966)
Big Wednesday, A Team Productions (US 1984)

The Endless Summer 2, Bruce Brown (US 1994)

magazines

Australian Surfing Life, PO Box 823, Burleigh Head, Queensland, 4220 Australia
Storm, c/o Low Pressure, 186 Kensington Park Road, London W11 1EF
Stormrider Guide to Europe – available from Low Pressure (see *Storm* above)
Surfing, Western Empire Publications Inc., 950 Calle Amanecer, Suite C, San Clemente, CA 92672, USA
Warp (surf and skate), 353 Airport Road, Oceanside, CA 92054, USA

mods

selected reading

Barnes, Richard, *Mods!*, London, 1991.
Cohn, Nik, 'Today There Are No Gentlemen', in *Ball the Wall*, London, 1989.
Chenoune, Farid, *A History of Men's Fashion*, Paris, 1993.
Connikie, Yvonne, *Fashions of a Decade: The 1960s*, London, 1990.
Fountain, Nigel, 'We're Different from the Average Person', *Observer Magazine* (2 September 1979): 36–41.
Franklin, Caryn, 'Style Wars', in *The i-D Bible: Every Ultimate Victim's Handbook*, London, n.d.
Godfrey, John, 'Acid Jazz Mods', *i-D* 75 (November 1989): 70–71.
—, 'Post-Modernism', *The Face* 2/28 (January 1991): 54–59.
Hebdige, Dick, 'Putting on the Style', *Time Out* (17 August 1979): 14–17.
—, *Subculture: The Meaning of Style*, London, 1979.
Lobenthal, Joel, *Radical Rags: Fashions of the Sixties*, New York, 1990.
MacInnes, Colin, *Absolute Beginners*, London, 1959.
Melly, George, *Revolt into Style*, Oxford, 1989.
Pearce, Chris, *The Sixties: A Pictorial Review*, London, n.d.

music

Booker T & the MGs, *Green Onions* (1962)
The Impressions, *You Ought To Be In Heaven* (1966)
John Lee Hooker, *Dimples* (1964)
Smith, Jimmy, *Got My Mojo Working* (1966)
Smokey Robinson & the Miracles, *Going To A Go–Go* (1966)

films

Up the Junction, Peter Collinson (GB 1967)
Quadrophenia, Franc Roddam (GB 1979)
Absolute Beginners, Julien Temple (GB 1986)

magazines

The Untouchables (and other Mod newsletters and magazines) available from Merc shop, 17/21 Ganton Street, London W1V 1LA

rockers

selected reading

Clay, Mike, *Café Racers: Rockers, Rock 'N' Roll and the Coffee-Bar Cult*, London, 1988.
Dunn, Nell, *Up the Junction*, London, 1963.

Farren, Mick, *The Black Leather Jacket*, London, 1985.

Hebdige, Dick, *Subculture: The Meaning of Style*, London, 1979.

McClellan, Jim, 'Rockers', *The Face* 2/25 (October 1990): 100–103.

Stuart, Johnny, *Rockers!*, London, 1987.

music

Johnny Kidd & the Pirates, *Shakin' All Over* (1960)

Sarne, Mike, *Just For Kicks* (1963)

The Ventures, *Two Thousand Pound Bee* (1964)

Taylor, Vince, *Brand New Cadillac* (1976)

Gene Vincent & the Blue Caps, *Be Bop A Lula* (1956)

films

The Wild One, Laslo Benedek (US 1954)

The Leather Boys, Sidney J. Furie (GB 1963)

magazines

Link (59 Club magazine, see below)

organizations

The 59 Club, c/o The Rectory, 19 Abbey Street, Plaistow, London E13 8DT

rude boys & two-tone

selected reading

Chambers, Iain, *Urban Rhythms: Pop Music and Popular Culture*, London, 1985.

Hebdige, Dick, *Cut 'N' Mix: Culture, Identity and Caribbean Music*, London, 1987.

—, *Subculture: The Meaning of Style*, London, 1979.

Marshall, George, *The Two Tone Story*, Dunoon, Scotland, 1992.

Thrills, Adrian, '2-Tone: End of Phase One', *The Face* 1 (May 1980): 4–11.

Tulloch, Carol, 'Rebel without a Pause: Black Streetstyle & Black Designers', in Julia Ash and Elizabeth Wilson, eds, *Chic Thrills*, London, 1992.

music: rude boys

Prince Buster, *Al Capone* (1967)

Dekker, Desmond, *007* (1967)

Perry, Lee, *The Upsetter* (1969)

Bob Marley and The Wailers, *Rude Boys* (1965)

Morgan, Derrick, *Tougher Than Tough* (n.d.)

music: two-tone

Bad Manners, *Ne-Ne Na-Na Na-Na Nu-Nu* (1980)

The Beat, *Hands Off (She's Mine)* (1980)

Bodysnatchers, *Ruder Than You* (n.d.)

Madness, *One Step Beyond* (1979)

Special a.k.a, *Gangsters* (1979)

films

The Harder They Come, Perry Henzell (Jamaica 1972)

Dance Craze, Joe Massot (GB 1981)

Take It or Leave It, Dave Robinson (GB 1981)

This Is Ska, Island Records (GB 1989)

swinging london & the psychedelics

selected reading

Lobenthal, Joel, *Radical Rags: Fashions of the Sixties*, New York, 1990.

Melly, George, *Revolt into Style*, Oxford, 1989.

Perry, Paul, *On the Bus: The Complete*

Guide to the Legendary Trip of Ken Kesey and the Merry Pranksters and the Birth of the Counterculture, London, 1990.

Powell, Polly, and Peel, Lucy, *'50s & '60s Style*, London, 1988.

Salter, Tom, *Carnaby Street*, Walton-on-Thames, 1970.

Thorne, Tony, *Fads, Fashions & Cults: From Acid House to Zoot Suit*, London, 1993.

Wolfe, Tom, *The Electric Kool-Aid Acid Test*, New York, 1968.

music: swinging london

The Action, *I'll Keep On Holding On* (1966)

Davy Jones & the Lower Third (Bowie), *You've Got A Habit Of Leaving* (1965)

The Kinks, *Dedicated Follower Of Fashion* (1966)

The Small Faces, *Whatcha Gonna Do About It?* (1965)

The Who, *My Generation* (1965)

music: psychedelics

Auger Trinity, Brian, *Tiger* (1967)

The Creation, *Painter Man* (1966)

Pink Floyd, *Interstellar Overdrive* (1968)

Traffic, *Am I What I Was Or Was I What I Am* (1968)

The Yardbirds, *Mister You're A Better Man Than I* (1966)

films

Blow Up, Michelangelo Antonioni (GB 1966)

Alfie, Lewis Gilbert (GB 1966)

Smashing Time, Desmond Davis (GB 1967)

Here We Go Round the Mulberry Bush, Clive Donner (GB 1967)

Tonite Let's All Make Love in London, Peter Whitehead (GB 1967)

The Jokers, Michael Winner (GB 1967)

hippies

selected reading

Cohn, Nik, 'Today There Are No Gentlemen', in *Ball the Wall*, London, 1989.

Darling, Andy, and Godfrey, John, 'Hippy Ever After', *i-D* 65 (December 1988/January 1989): 20–31.

Lobenthal, Joel, *Radical Rags: Fashions of the Sixties*, New York, 1990.

Perry, Paul, *On the Bus: The Complete Guide to the Legendary Trip of Ken Kesey and the Merry Pranksters and the Birth of the Counterculture*, London, 1990.

Sandford, Jeremy, and Reid, Ron, *Tomorrow's People*, London, 1974.

Wolfe, Tom, *The Electric Kool-Aid Acid Test*, New York, 1968.

music

The Byrds, *Eight Miles High* (1966)

Crosby, Stills, Nash &Young, *Woodstock* (1970)

Grateful Dead, *Terrapin Station* (1977)

Jefferson Airplane, *White Rabbit* (1967)

Joplin, Janis, *Down On Me* (1972)

films

Easy Rider, Dennis Hopper (US 1969)

Woodstock, Michael Wadleigh (US 1970)

greasers

selected reading

Farren, Mick, *The Black Leather Jacket*, London, 1985.

Perry, Paul, *On the Bus: The Complete Guide to the Legendary Trip of Ken Kesey and the Merry Pranksters and the Birth of the Counterculture*, London, 1990.

Stuart, Johnny, *Rockers!*, London, 1987.

music

Bobby Fuller Four, *I Fought The Law* (1966)

Nashville Teens, *Tobacco Road* (1964)

The Rolling Stones, *Paint It Black* (1966)

Surfaris, *Wipe Out* (1963)

Wild Angels, *Nervous Breakdown* (1968)

films

The Wild Angels, Roger Corman (US 1966)

Easy Rider, Dennis Hopper (US 1969)

magazines

Easy Rider, PO Box 390, Mount Morris, IL 61054, USA

skinheads

selected reading

Barnes, Richard, *Mods!*, London, 1991.

Franklin, Caryn, 'Style Wars', in *The i-D Bible: Every Ultimate Victim's Handbook*, London, n.d.

Hebdige, Dick, *Subculture: The Meaning of Style*, London, 1979.

Johnson, Garry, *The Story of Oi*, Manchester, n.d.

Knight, Nick, *Skinhead*, London, 1982.

Marshall, George, *Spirit of '69: A Skinhead Bible*, Dunoon, Scotland, 1991.

music

The Business, *Harry May* (1980)

Dekker, Desmond, *The Israelites* (1969)

Madness, *One Step Beyond* (1979)

The Pioneers, *Long Shot Kick De Bucket* (1969)

Special a.k.a., *Gangsters* (1979)

films

Clockwork Orange, Stanley Kubrick (GB 1971)

Romper Stomper, Geoffrey Wright (Australia 1992)

magazines

Skinhead Times, S. T. Publishing, PO Box 12, Dunoon, Argyll PA23 7BQ, Scotland

funk

selected reading

Beard, Steve, and McClellan, Jim, 'Blaxploitation', *i-D* 54 (December 1987): 58–59.

Milner, Christina and Richard, *Black Players: The Secret World of Black Pimps*, London, 1972.

Pickin, Marc, 'Funk Rocks Funk Rock Funk Rock', *i-D* 109 (October 1992): 22–27.

Witter, Simon, 'Parliafunkadelicment!', *i-D* 58 (May 1988): 90–93, 112.

Wolfe, Tom, 'Funky Chic', in *Mauve Gloves & Madmen, Clutter & Vine*, New York, 1977.

music

Brown, James, *Sex Machine* (1970)

General Crook, *Fever In The Funkhouse* (1974)

Ohio Players, *Fire* (1973)

Parliament, *Up For The Downstroke* (1974)

War, *Me And Baby Brother* (1976)

films

Shaft, Gordon Parks (US 1971)

Superfly, Gordon Parks (US 1972)

glam

selected reading

Carr, Roy, and Shaar Murray, Charles, *Bowie: An Illustrated Record*, New York, 1981.

Thorne, Tony, *Fads, Fashions & Cults: From Acid House to Zoot Suit*, London, 1993.

Thorton, Phil, 'Flared to Death', *The Face* 2/19 (April 1990): 56–57.

Tobler, John, and Frame, Pete, *25 Years of Rock*, London, 1980.

music

Bowie, David, *Moonage Daydream* (1971)

Glitter, Gary, *I'm The Leader Of The Gang* (1973)

Steve Harley & the Cockney Rebel, *Make Me Smile (Come Up And See Me)* (1973)

Slade, *Coz I Luv You* (1971)

T. Rex, *Jeepster* (1971)

rastafarians

selected reading

Bergman, Billy, *Reggae & Latin Pop*, Poole, Dorset, 1985.

Hebdige, Dick, *Cut 'N' Mix: Culture, Identity and Caribbean Music*, London, 1987.

Thomas, Michael, and Boot, Adrian, *Jah Revenge: Babylon Revisited*, London, 1982.

Tulloch, Carol, 'Rebel without a Pause: Black Streetstyle & Black Designers', in Julia Ash and Elizabeth Wilson, eds, *Chic Thrills*, London, 1992.

music: roots/reggae

The Abbyssinians, *Satta Amassagana* (1969)

Dub Judah, *Babylon Is A Trap* (1992)

Junior Marvin, *Police & Thieves* (1976)

Max Romeo, *War In Babylon* (1976)

The Wailers, *Get Up, Stand Up* (1973)

headbangers

selected reading

Chambers, Iain, *Urban Rhythms: Pop Music and Popular Culture*, London, 1985.

Evans, Liz, 'The Death of Heavy Metal – The Reincarnation of Rock & Roll', *i-D* 73 (September 1989): 14–16.

Flett, Kathryn, 'Heavy: The i-Diots Guide to Heavy Metal', *i-D* 34 (March 1986): 72–74.

St Michael, Mick, *Heavy Metal*, London, 1992.

music

Bon Jovi, *Keep The Faith* (1992)

Deep Purple, *Highway Star* (1975)

Led Zeppelin, *When The Levee Breaks* (1974)

Lynyrd Skynyrd, *Free Bird* (1976)

Metallica, *Enter Sandman* (1991)

films

Easy Rider, Dennis Hopper (US 1969)

Woodstock, Michael Wadleigh (US 1970)

The Song Remains the Same, Peter Clifton, Joe Massot (US 1976)

This Is Spinal Tap, Rob Reiner (US 1984)

magazines

DRZ, 44 Platts Road, Enfield, EN3 5NA

Kerrang! and *Raw*, Lisa House, 52–55 Carnaby Street, London W1V 1PF

northern soul

selected reading

Chambers, Iain, *Urban Rhythms: Pop Music and Popular Culture*, London, 1985.

Joye, Eddie, 'The First Bognor Soul Weekender', *i-D* 37 (June 1986): 78–80.

Rushton, Neil, 'Out on the Floor: A Primer for the New Soul Rebels', *The Face* 29 (September 1982): 18–23.

music

Carstairs, *It Really Hurts Me Girl* (1968/9)

Jones, Gloria, *Tainted Love* (n.d.)

Dave Mitchell and the Screamers, *The Trip* (1968/9)

The OJs, *Hold On* (1968/9)

The Salvadors, *Stick By Me Baby* (1968/9)

skaters

selected reading

Anon., 'Skate Like There's No Tomorrow', *i-D* 26 (June 1985): 30–33.

Anon., 'Skate and Destroy', *The Face* 76 (August 1986): 28–29.

Harpin, Lee, 'Fat!', *i-D* 114 (March 1993): 20–23.

Schaack, Sandy, 'Baggies', *i-D* 29 (September 1985): 28–29.

magazines

B-side, 18 rue Marcel Miguel, 92130 Issy-les-Moulineaux, France

Monster Mag, Friedrich-Ebert Str. 15, D4400 Münster, Germany

R.a.D., The Blue Barn, Tew Lane, Wooton, Woodstock, Oxon OX7 1HA

Thrasher, 1303 Underwood Ave., San Francisco, CA 94124, USA

Transworld Skateboarding, 353 Airport Road, Oceanside, CA 92033, USA

XXX Magazine, Via I Maggio 9, 22073 Fino Mornasco (CO), Italy

punks

selected reading

Anscombe, Isabelle, *Not Another Punk Book!*, London, 1978.

Bollon, Patrice, *Morale du Masque*, Paris, 1990.

Hebdige, Dick, *Subculture: The Meaning of Style*, London, 1979.

Hennessy, Val, *In the Gutter*, London, 1978.

Savage, Jon, 'The Punk Process', *The Face* 19 (November 1981): 48–54.

—, 'Punk', *The Face* 70 (February 1986): 40–53.

—, *England's Dreaming*, London, 1991.

Toulouse, Vaughn, 'My Life in Punk Rock: Siouxsie Sioux', *The Face* 4 (August 1980): 40–46.

Turbett, Virginia, 'Punk Rock 5 Years On', *The Face* 20 (December 1981): 46–47.

music

The Adverts, *Bored Teenagers* (1978)

The Clash, *White Riot* (1977)

Sex Pistols, *Anarchy In The UK* (1976)

Siouxsie and the Banshees, *Love In A Void* (n.d.)

X-Ray Spex, *Oh Bondage, Up Yours!* (1978)

films

Jubilee, Derek Jarman (GB 1978)

The Great Rock and Roll Swindle, Julien Temple (GB 1980)

new romantics

selected reading

Elms, Robert, 'The Cult with No Name', *The Face* 7 (November 1980): 22–27.

Johnson, David, '69 Dean Street', *The Face* 34 (February 1983): 26–31.

Savage, Jon, 'Brave New Twirl', *The Face* 12 (April 1981): 40–42.

Truman, James, 'Adam Ant and the Selling of Blitz Culture', *The Face* 15 (July 1981): 6–7.

York, Peter, *Style Wars*, London, 1980.

music

Fad Gadget, *Ricky's Hand* (1980)

The Human League, *Being Boiled* (1982)

Kraftwerk, *Showroom Dummy* (1982)

Newman, Gary, *Are Friends Electric* (1979)

Visage, *Fade To Grey* (1980)

goths

selected reading

Heath, Ashley, 'The Return of Goth?', *The Face* 2/56 (May 1993): 37.

Johnson, David, 'Beyond the Batcave', *The Face* 46 (February 1984): 28–29.

—, '69 Dean Street', *The Face* 34 (February 1983): 26–31.

Mercer, Mick, *Gothic Rock*, Birmingham, 1991.

music

Bauhaus, *Bela Lugosi's Dead* (1979)

The Cure, *The Funeral Party* (n.d.)

The Damned, *Sanctum Sanctorum* (n.d.)

Siouxsie and the Banshees, *Happy House* (1980)

Sisters of Mercy, *This Corrosion* (1987)

films

The Cabinet of Dr Caligari, Robert Wiene (Germany 1919)

Nosferatu, F. W. Murnau (Germany 1921)

Nosferatu the Vampyre, Werner Herzog (West Germany/France 1979)

The Hunger, Tony Scott (US 1983)

Gothic, Ken Russell (GB 1986)

The Addams Family, Barry Sonnenfeld (US 1991)

magazines

Bats and Red Velvet, 47 Cavendish Place, Newcastle upon Tyne, England

Propaganda/The Dead Are Also Suspended/Necropolis, PO Box 296, New Hide Park, New York 11040, USA

Velvet Vampyre (see *Vampyre Society* below)

organizations

The Gothic Society, 138 Canterbury Road, Harrow, Middlesex HA1 4PB (Nosferatu's Fan Club)

The Vampyre Society, PO Box 68, Keighley, West Yorkshire BD22

casuals

selected reading

Allen, Vaughan, 'Faking It', *The Face* 2/23 (August 1990): 40–43.

Elms, Robert, 'A Celebration of World Football', *The Face* 2/20 (May 1990): 39–45.

Harpin, Lee, 'Boys Will Be Boys', *i-D* 109 (October 1992): 10–13.

Hills, Gavin, and Benson, Richard,

'Casuals', *The Face* 2/59 (August 1993): 94–100.

Sampson, Kevin, and Rimmer, Dave, 'The Ins and Outs of High Street Fashion', *The Face* 39 (July 1983): 22–25.

psychobillies

music

Fenech, Paul, *The Rocking Dead* (1993)

The Meteors, *Wrecking Crew* (1982)

The Meteors, *Psycho Cat* (1987)

The Meteors, *Chainsaw Boogie* (1993)

The Meteors, *Hell Ain't Hot Enough* (1994)

films

The Texas Chainsaw Massacre, Tobe Hooper (US 1975)

Meteor Madness, Palace Pictures (GB 1981)

organizations

The Voice Of The Bell (Meteors' Fan Club), PO Box 1556, Swindon, Wiltshire SN1 1ZA

pervs

selected reading

Olley, Michelle, 'We're All Going on a Kinky Holiday', *i-D* 90 (March 1991): 36–39.

Polhemus, Ted, and Randall, Housk, *Rituals of Love: Sexual Experiments, Erotic Possibilities*, London, 1994.

Randall, Housk, *Revelations: Chronicles and Visions from the Sexual Underworld*, London, 1993.

Russell Powell, Fiona, 'Bent for Leather', *The Face* (October 1983): 60–64.

Thompson, Mark, *Leatherfolk*, Boston, Mass., 1991.

films

Maîtresse, Barbet Schroeder (France 1976)

Mano Destra, Cleo Uebellmann (Switzerland 1986)

Rubber Ball, Skin Two (GB 1992)

magazines

Demonia, Societé Comedit, 15 Cité Joly, 75011 Paris, France

Fetish Times, KP Publishing, BCM Box 6883, London WC1N 3XX

O, Tech Com, Kronprinzenstr 30, 42630 Solingen, Germany

Ritual, P&P, 29 Brewer St, London W1R 3FE

Sandmutopia Guardian & Dungeon Journal, Desmodus Inc., PO Box 410390, San Francisco, CA 94141-0390, USA

Skin Two, Tim Woodward Publishing Ltd, BCM Box 2071, London WC1N 3XX

b-boys & flygirls

selected reading

Anon., 'Rap Payback – Past and Present', *i-D* 79 (February 1990): 68–73.

Adler, B. and Beckman, Janette, *RAP!*, London, 1991.

Collin, Matthew, 'One Nation under a Groove', *i-D* 68 (April 1989): 20–23.

Cooper, Carol, 'Run for It', *The Face* 55 (November 1984): 41–43.

Elms, Robert, 'Bronx Breakout!', *The Face* 31 (November 1982): 76–77.

Garratt, Sheryl, 'Flatbush City Limits', *The Face* 78 (October 1986): 58–64.

Toop, David, and Rambali, Paul, 'Electro', *The Face* 49 (May 1984): 40–49.

Toop, David, *The Rap Attack: African Jive to New York Hip Hop*, London, 1984.

—, 'Yo! Homeboy: Into the Krush Groove', *The Face* 70 (February 1986): 10–16.

music

Dr Dre, *G-Thang* (1992)

EPMD, *So Watcha Sayin* (1988)

Grandmaster Flash & the Furious Five, *The Adventures Of* (1982)

Run DMC, *Peter Piper* (1986)

Ultramagnetic MC's, *Chorus Line* (1990)

films

Beat Street, Stan Lathan (US 1984)

Breakdance (US title: *Breakin'*), Joel Silberg (US 1984)

Krush Groove, Michael Schultz (US 1985)

Do the Right Thing, Spike Lee (US 1989)

Boyz N the Hood, John Singleton (US 1991)

magazines

Hip Hop Connection, Popular Publications, Alexander House, Forehill, Ely, Cambs. CB7 4AF

The Source, PO Box 586, Mount Morris, IL 61054, USA

Vibe, 205 Lexington Ave., 3rd Floor, New York, NY 10016, USA

Represent, Represent House, Woodhall, Wigton CA7 8JT

Echoes, 79 Charlotte Street, London W1P 1HD

MixMag, PO Box 89, London W14 8ZW

raggamuffins & bhangra style

selected reading

Ablett, Paul, 'The Ragamuffin Queen', *i-D* 73 (September 1989): 53–54.

Allen, Vaughan, 'Bhangramuffin', *The Face* 2/44 (May 1992): 104–108.

Cosgrove, Stuart, 'Ragamuffin Rap', *The Face* 97 (May 1988): 66–68.

Datar, Rajan, 'Dread Indian', *The Face* 2/32 (May 1991): 60–61.

Dewan, Veeno, 'Crash Bhangra Wallop!', *i-D* 59 (June 1988): 72–76.

Eshun, Kodwo, 'Rebel Music', *i-D* 111 (December 1992): 6–10.

Harpin, Lee, 'General Levy', *The Face* 2/54 (March 1993): 100–105.

Hebdige, Dick, *Cut 'N' Mix: Culture, Identity and Caribbean Music*, London, 1987.

Jahn, Brian, and Weber, Tom, *Reggae Island: Jamaican Music in the Digital Age*, Kingston, 1992.

McCann, Ian, 'Bhangramuffin!', *i-D* 115 (April 1993): 16–21.

music: ragga

Buju Banton, *Murderer* (1992)

Cutty Ranks, *The Stopper* (1990)

The Pinchers, *Si Mi Ya* (1992)

Smith, Wayne, *Under Me Sleng Teng* (n.d.)

Yellowman, *Nobody Move* (1993)

music: bhangra

Alaap, *Dance With Alaap* (1984)

Apache Indian, *No Reservations* (1993)

Balisagoo, *Essential Ragga* (1992)

Hustlers HC, *Big Trouble In Little Asia* (1993)

Satrang, *Never Mind The Dholaks* (1991)

magazines

Touch, Studio 606, 8 Nursery Road, London SW9 8BP

new age travellers
selected reading
Lowe, Richard, and Shaw, William, *Travellers*, London, 1993.
Marcus, Tony, 'Summer of Chaos', *The Face* 119 (August 1993): 78–90.
Moir, Jan, 'Caravan: On the Road Again', *Weekend Guardian* (22–23 August 1992).
Raphael, Amy, 'Road Runners', *The Face* 2/47 (August 1992): 96–103.
Rosenberger, Alex, 'Life on the Road', *Festival Eye* 4 (Summer 1989): 34–37.
music
Hawkwind, *Silver Machine* (1973)
The Levellers, *This Garden* (1993)
New Model Army, *Heroin* (1984)
Ozric Tentacles, *Jurassic Shift* (1993)
Senser, *No Comply* (1994)
films
Operation Solstice, Gareth Morris (GB 1991, Channel 4)
magazines
POD – PO Box 23, London SE4 1S
Ptolemaic Terrascope, 37 Sandridge Road, Melksham, Wiltshire SN12 7BQ

ravers
selected reading
Allen, Vaughan, 'The Manchester Effect', *The Face,* 2/25 (October 1990): 84–91.
Foote, Jennifer, 'Madchester!', *Newsweek* 4 (23 July 1990): 44–49.
'London vs Manchester', various authors, *The Face* 2/18 (March 1990): 60–75.
Macpherson, Don, 'Holiday Babylon', *The Face* 65 (September 1985): 34–44.
Garratt, Sheryl, 'Chicago House', *The Face* 77 (September 1986): 18–23.
Nevin, Charles, 'Made in Manchester', *Weekend Guardian* (15–16 June 1991).
Noon, Mike, 'Freaky Dancing', *i-D* 77 (February 1990): 46–48.
Redhead, Steve, *The End-of-the-Century Party*, Manchester, 1990.
music
Altern 8, *Evaporate* (1992)
Leftfield, *Open Up* (n.d.)
Prodigy, *Charly* (1991)
SL2, *DJs Take Control* (1991)
films
Young Americans, Danny Cannon (GB 1993)
Shopping, Paul Anderson (GB 1994)
magazines
MixMag, PO Box 89, London W14 8ZW

acid jazz
selected reading
Godfrey, John, 'Acid Jazz', *i-D* 60 (July 1988): 74–76.
music
Brand New Heavies, *Dream Come True* (1992)
DJ Shadow, *In Flux* (1994)
Frisk, *Take The Sun Away* (1994)
Galliano, *Jus' Rech* (1992)
Young Disciples, *Apparently Nothin'* (1991)
magazines
Straight No Chaser, 41 Coronet St, London N1 6HD
Vibe, 205 Lexington Avenue, 3rd Floor, New York, NY 10016, USA

indie kids, cuties, grunge & riot grrrls
selected reading
Daly, Steven, 'Boston, Campus Grunge', *The Face* 2/50 (November 1992): 130–134.
—, 'Sub Pop Culture', *The Face* 2/47 (August 1992): 90–95.
Raphael, Amy 'Hole Lotta Love', *The Face* 2/53 (February 1993): 34–43.
Redhead, Steve, *The End-of-the-Century Party*, Manchester, 1990.
music: indie kids
The Happy Mondays, *Wrote For Luck* (1988)
Joy Division, *Transmission* (1981)
The Smiths, *Panic* (1986)
Stone Roses, *Fool's Gold* (1989)
The Wonder Stuff, *The Size Of A Cow* (1991)
music: grunge
Dinosaur Jr, *Start Chopping* (1993)
Hole, *My Beautiful Son* (n.d.)
Nirvana, *Smells Like Teen Spirit* (1991)
Pearl Jam, *Jeremy* (1992)
Soundgarden, *Rusty Cage* (1993)
films
Slacker, Richard Linklater (US 1991)
Singles, Cameron Crowe (US 1992)
magazines
Blag, 77 James St, Louth LN11 0JR
Melody Maker, IPC, King's Reach Tower, Stamford St, London SE1 9LS
NME, 1061 Oakfield House, Perrymount Rd, Haywards Heath, West Sussex RH16 3ZA
Select, Mappin House, 4 Winsley St, London W1N 5AR
Submerge, 35 Lickey House, North End Road, London W9 9UQ
Katatonic, 56 Spencer Road, Twickenham, Middx TW2 5TQ
Girl Frenzy, PO Box 148, Hove, East Sussex BN3 3DQ

technos & cyberpunks
selected reading
Collin, Matthew, 'Techno Is the Sound of Europe', *i-D* 99 (December 1991): 18–23.
Heley, Mark, 'Cyberspace – The Final Frontier', *i-D* 76 (December 1989): 36–39.
Hills, Gavin, 'Tekkno City', *The Face* 41 (February 1992): 70–74.
Hoskyns, Barney, 'King of the Cybermen', *Vogue* (October 1993): 214–217.
McClellan, Jim, 'Futura Shock', *The Face* 2/45 (June 1992): 88–89.
—, 'The Man Who Made Cyberspace', *The Face* 2/61 (October 1993): 62–66.
McCready, John, 'A-Z of Techno', *The Face* 2/39 (December 1991): 54–59.
music
Bowie, David, *Jump* (1993)
The Cocteau Twins, *Pearly Dewdrops Drops* (1984)
Front 242, *Headhunter* (1988)
Nitzer Ebb, *Let Your Body Learn* (1986)
Ministry, *Jesus Built My Hot Rod* (1991)
films
Blade Runner, Ridley Scott (US 1982)
Videodrome, David Cronenberg (Canada 1983)

Robocop, Paul Verhoeven (US 1987)
Gunhed, Masato Harada (Japan 1989)
magazines
DJ, Orpheus Publications, 4th Floor, Centrehouse, Mandela Street, London NW1 0DU
Driver, Chromium Palace, 8 Holmdale Road, London NW6 1BP
MixMag, PO Box 89, London W14 8ZW
G Spot, 11 Marshalsea Road, London SE1 1EP
Mondo 2000, PO Box 40271, Berkeley, CA 94704, USA

the gathering of the tribes
selected reading
Collin, Matthew, 'Turn on, Tune in, Sort It Out', *Observer Life Magazine* (5 December 1993): 4–6.
Godfrey, John, 'Hippy Hour', *i-D* 82 (July 1990): 68–79.
Scott, Danny, 'Festivals!', *The Face* 2/56 (May 1993): 56–63.
Sharkey, Alix, 'New Tribes of England', *Guardian Weekend* (11 December 1993): 38–46.
magazines
Dream Creation Inc., 108 Lady Margaret Rd., London N19 5EX
Head, BM Uplift, London WC1N 3XX

the supermarket of style
selected reading
Redhead, Steve, *The End-of-the-Century Party,* Manchester, 1990.
Sharkey, Alix, 'New Tribes of England', *Guardian Weekend* (11 December 1993): 38–46.
Wakefield, Neville, *Postmodernism: The Twilight of the Real,* London, 1990.
magazines
Cutie Magazine, 5-5-5 Koji-Machi, Chiyoda-ku, Tokyo, Japan T102
Dazed & Confused and *Another Magazine,* 2nd Floor, 56 Brewer St., London W1
The Face, 3rd Floor, Block A, Exmouth House, Pine St, London EC1R 0JL
i-D, Universal House, 251-255 Tottenham Court Road, London W1P 0AB
Positive Energy of Madness, 1 Hazlemere, Rydens Rd., Walton-on-Thames, Surrey KT12 3AQ

Ace Records 27, 41; Acid Jazz Records 120 bottom; Janette Beckman 58, 59, 60 right, 73 top, 106, 107 left, right and below; BFI 4, 18 bottom, 23, 26, 31 left, 44, 45 left, 47, 72; BMG Records (UK) Ltd 24 top left and centre, 74 left, 75 left; Camera Press (Ron Reid) 64 left; Castle Communications 80 bottom; © William Claxton 39; Colorific! 50; David Corio 24 top right, 25 left, 42 left, 73 left, 76, 77, 79 above left, 108 above and below, 109; *Cutie* magazine 130 right, 133 top right; Deram Records Group 51, 52 left; Dovetail Records (Photo Pat Sheehan) 114 top; © 8-Track Cartridge Family 75; Simon Fowler 120 top; Fox Brothers Tailors of Chicago 29 left; Kate Garner 111 below; Sally and Richard Greenhill Photo Library 78 right; Courtesy of Martin Heaphy 32 centre, 37 left; Hulton Deutsch Collection Ltd 6, 21, 22, 31 right, 33, 46, 65 right, 67, 68, 114 bottom; © *i-D* magazine 88 left; Island Records 111 bottom (Photo Kate Garner); Courtesy of Mandy Jarman 71 right; Nick Knight (from *Skinhead,* Omnibus Press, 1982) 69 right; Tim Leighton Boyce 86, 87 left and bottom right, 88 bottom; Lewis Leathers 10 left; Ted Polhemus 2, 8 right, 10 right, 13 top and bottom, 15, 18 top, 36 left, 43 right, 53 right, 57 left, 60 top, 61 right, 63, 66 right, 70 left and right, 81 left and right, 82 left, 82 right, 83 left, centre and right, 90 top and bottom, 91 top right, 92, 93 top, 94 left and right, 95 left and right, 96 left and right, 97 left, 98 left, 99 top and bottom right, 103 top and bottom left, 104 top centre, 113 left, 116 right, 130 top, 131; Popperfoto 7, 34 left, 54, 62 left; © Steve Pyke 35, 53 left, 127; Redferns 28, 38 top; Rex Features 74 right; Courtesy Zandra Rhodes Designs (Photo Clive Arrowsmith) 8 below; © Skin Two 104 below, 105 below; © Paul Slattery 102 top; Talkin' Loud (Photo Simon Fowler) 120 top; Wolfgang Tillmans Courtesy Interim Art London 110 top left, 111 top, 126; Topham 40; Trojan Records Ltd 78 top left; Roger Viollet 20; Gavin Watson (Printed by Cass) 14, 71 top left, 91 below.

acknowledgments

This book has relied heavily on the advice, criticism and goodwill of a wide network of people who have a personal, long-standing interest in specific subcultures. While I alone accept ultimate responsibility for the views and information in *Streetstyle*, without their generous help this book would have been impossible. I hope they feel that their input has been treated fairly and accurately. Those listed below with an asterisk* after their names have provided or contributed to the music lists which appear in the Further Information section.

zooties: Anne Adeyemi, Yve N'Goo, Chris Sullivan* (Wag Club), Judy Westacott **zazous**: Natalie Bishop-Lemercier* **caribbean style**: Jonathan Fleming, Sue Steward **western style**: Deborah King* and Adam Sanderson of Lonesome No More, Judy Westacott **bikers**: Judy Westacott **hip cats & hipsters**: Chris Sullivan* **beats, beatniks & existentialists**: Sarah Callard, Carolyn Cassady **teddy boys**: Dixie Coombs, Susie Diamonds and Ritchie Gee of T.E.D.S., Martin Heaphy*, Judy Westacott **modernists**: Sarah Callard, Chris Sullivan **folkies**: Sarah Callard, Bob Davenport* **rockabillies**: Jay Strongman*, Judy Westacott **la dolce vita**: Mike Ferrante, Giannino Malossi, Betti Marenco **coffee-bar cowboys & ton-up boys**: Shaun John, Rick Parkington, Johnny Stuart, Judy Westacott **surfers**: Caroline Greville-Morris, Low Pressure **mods**: Andy Clarke, Mike Ferrante* **rockers**: Johnny Stuart, Judy Westacott* **rude boys & two-tone**: Yve N'Goo, Gaz Mayall*, Shaun Cole **swinging london & the psychedelics**: Mike Ferrante*, Sarah Miller (West Soho Ass.) **hippies**: Ron Reid* **greasers**: Peter Bruce*, Johnny Stuart, Judy Westacott **skinheads**: Shaun Cole, Mandy Jarman, Gavin Watson* **funk**: Yve N'Goo, Susan Shaw (*The South Bank Show*) **glam**: Faebhean Kwest* **rastafarians**: Anne Adeyemi, Mathew Dean*, Damien Marty*, Yve N'Goo **headbangers**: Kate Webb* **northern soul**: Keb Darge*, Will Hoon, Mark Wigan **skaters**: Tim Leighton-Boyce, Elsa Rand, Slam City Skates **punks**: Joe Brocklehurst, Louise Cain, Philip Sallon*, George O'Dowd*, Betti Marenco **new romantics**: Philip Sallon*, George O'Dowd* **goths**: Pandora Gorey*, Patricia Morrison **casuals**: Justin Alphonse, Will Hoon **psychobillies**: Ray Hare, Joe DeCastro, Michelle Fenech*, Judy Westacott **pervs**: Housk Randall, Tim Woodward and Tony Mitchel of Skin Two **b-boys & fly girls**: Anne Adeyemi, Jonathan Fleming, Yve N'Goo, Normsky (*Dance Energy*), Mark Polack, Simon King-Underwood, Bill Wake* (Jam Record Shop, Newcastle) **raggamuffins**: Anne Adeyemi, Jonathan Fleming, Yve N'Goo*, Mark Polack, Bill Wake* **bhangra style**: Ray and Matthew of Bombay Jungle (Wag Club), Cally (Island Records) **new age travellers**: Sarah Callard, Robbie Crow, Jeremy Deller* **ravers**: Sarah Callard, Fiona Cartledge*, Jeremy Deller*, Steve Lazarides, James Matheson, David Swindells **acid jazz**: Paul Bradshaw (*Straight No Chaser*), Adam Friedman, Emma Goodman, Steve Lazarides* **indie kids & grunge**: Sarah Callard, Jeremy Deller* **technos & cyberpunks**: Lee Newman, Xaiüla Xavaar* (*Driver* magazine) **the gathering of the tribes**: Sarah Callard, Alix Sharkey, David Swindells **the supermarket of style**: Clare Carnegie, Fiona Cartledge, *Dazed and Confused*, Jeremy Deller, Gavin Fernandes, James Matheson, Norbert Schoerner, Alix Sharkey, Mark Wigan

Nor would this book have been possible without the help, goodwill and skill of those photographers whose work appears in it. Thanks too to all of those who have posed for them (and for me) and to Sarah Tierney who collaborated with me on many photo expeditions.

The research and writing of this book coincided with my serving as the External Curator to the Victoria and Albert Museum's STREETSTYLE exhibition (November 1994). Although separate projects, the overlap of subject matter greatly enhanced the scope of research for both text and photographs. I am, therefore, grateful to the V&A for taking up my original proposal for this exhibition and to all those who have provided practical help, encouragement and constructive criticism – in particular Linda Lloyd Jones, Lesley Woodbridge, Francesca Mills, Alison Pearce (Exhibitions); Tracy Williamson, Pippa Grimes, Robyn Griffith-Jones, Robin Cole-Hamilton (Marketing); Sharon Beard, Colin Corbett, Brian Griggs (Design); Shaun Cole (Prints and Drawings). Photographic research for the V&A by Sarah Callard (with Justin Alphonse and Simon King-Underwood) was vital in tracking down many of the photographers whose work appears here. Research reports on various styletribes prepared by Sarah Callard, Jonathan Fleming, Pandora Gorey, Will Hoon, Steve Lazarides, Judy Westacott and others for the V&A provided much needed background information. The views expressed in this book are my own and not necessarily those of the V&A's staff.

General theoretic advice and feedback was provided by (among others): Buster and Pris, Giulia Ceriani (C.R.A., Milan), Ian Chambers (University of Naples), Roberto Grandi (University of Bologna), Annmaree Kealy, Jose Kemp and Maria Costantino (Epsom College of Art and Design), Dominic Lutyens, Giannino Malossi (Pitti Immagine, Florence), Betti Marenco, Fabio and Renato Molho, Norbert Schoerner and Mark Wigan.

Extra special thanks to Fiona Cartledge (Sign of the Times) for her formidable Filofax and to Claudia Pastuszynski and Koji Yamashita of Total Art Co. (Tokyo).

Heartfelt thanks to my family and friends for their patience and encouragement.

Betti Marenco drew the Streetstyle flowchart, assisted with the final revision of the text and the last stage of picture research, and helped to compile the Further Information section.

index

Absolute Beginners 50, 51
Ace Café, London 46, 47, 55
acid house 115, 116, 124; *117*
Acid Jazz 53, 118-121; *118-21*
Afrocentric style 108; *107*
Aitken, Laurel 58; *58*
Apache Indian 111; *111*
Armstrong, Louis 38
Autry, Gene 25
Avengers, The (TV) 63, 103

B-Boys 106-8; *106-8*
Baker, Chet 44
'Baldricks' 116
Baudrillard, Jean 7
Bay City Rollers 85
Beach Boys, the 48
Beatniks 31-2, 40; *31, 32*
Beats 29, 30-2, 40, 48, 64, 66, 112; *30, 32*
bebop (music) 28, 38, 118
bebop (style) 28-9
Bedazzled, Clara 75
Bhangra 110, 111
Bikers 26-7, 48, 67-8; *27*
Black Sabbath 80
Bloggs, Joe 116; *117*
Blow Up (film) 63
blue beat 69
Bolan, Marc 63, 75
Booker T & the MGs 52
Bowie, David 75; *74*
Boy George 79, 95; *96*
Bracknell Chopper Club 13; *13*
Brando, Marlon 10, 26, 27; *26*
break-dancing 106; *108*
Bronx jacket *see* Perfecto jacket
bubble-up effect 10, 12

Calloway, Cab 19, 28, 29; *18*
Caribbean style 21-2; *21*
Carnaby Street, London 52, 61, 62, 63; *51, 62*
Casely-Hayford, Joe 12
Cassady, Carolyn 30
Cassady, Neal 30, 63; *30*
Casuals 100-101, 116; *100, 101*
Chantays, The 48
Charles, Ray 52
Chenoune, Farid 20
Cliff, Jimmy *72*
Clinton, George 63, 73, 75; *73*
Cochran, Eddie 57
Coffee-bar Cowboys 46-7, 55
Cohen, 'Nudie' 24
Cohn, Nik 52
Collins, Bootsy 63, 73, 75; *73*
Cool School, The *see* Modernists
Cool School jazz 51
Cosmic Crusader 75
country and western (music) 23, 24, 25, 42
Cuties 122; *123*
Cyberpunks 63, 125, 127; *124, 125, 127*
Cycle Savages, The (film) 67

Daltrey, Roger 53
Davis, Miles 31, 38, 39
Dean, James 41
Dekker, Desmond 59
denim 24, 43, 68, 80, 83, 102, 110, 116; *80, 82-3*
Dior, Christian 9, 10
DIY leather jacket art *10, 83, 90*

Dr Martens (boots) 92, 102, 122; *69, 102*
Dolce Vita, La (film) 45
Dolce Vita, La (style) 44-5
Donga Tribe, The 129; *129*
dreadlocks 76-8
Dressing Down 17, 24, 43, 73, 96, 122, 123
Dressing Up 17, 19, 43, 72, 116
Dunstable Tattoo Festival 13; *13, 102*

Easy Rider (film) 68, 112
'Eco' movement 114
Ecstasy 101, 115, 116
Edwardian Drape Society, The (T.E.D.S.) 131; *16*
Egan, Rusty 95, 96
Eldridge, Roy 29
Elle (magazine) 12
Erik B. & Rakim 108
ethnic influence 65, 66, 113; *65, 66*
Evans, Gil 38, 39
Existentialists 31, 40
Expresso Bongo (film) 32

Face, The (magazine) 12, 96, 100
Farren, Mick 26, 29
Fellini, Federico 45
fetishism 92, 103, 104, 105
59 Club 67; *55, 56*
Flower Power 66
Flügel, J. C. 18
Flygirls 106-8; *107*
folk music 40
Folkies 40, 48, 49, 64, 66; *40*
football (stadium) fashion 100, 101
42nd Street (film) 6-7
Freaks 65, 66, 113
Funk 66, 72-3, 75, 118; *72, 73*
Fury, Billy 57

Gaillard, Slim 30
Galliano, John 99
Galliano, Rob 118
Gaultier, Jean-Paul 11; *25, 125*
Gaye, Marvin 52
Gillespie, Dizzy 28, 29, 38; *29*
Glam (Rock) 66, 74-5, 83, 97; *74, 75*
Glastonbury Festival *113, 123*
Goldberg, Joe 38, 39
gospel music 42
Goths 75, 97-9; *97-99*
Grandmaster Flash 106, 107
Greasers 67-8; *67, 68*
'Great Masculine Renunciation' 18
Greco, Juliette 31
Greenpeace 114
Grunge 88, 122; *123*

Haley, Bill 34, 36
Hamnett, Katharine 11; *11, 37*
Harder They Come, The (film) 72
Harlem, New York 21, 28; *28*
Havana, Cuba 21
Headbangers 80-3; *80*
Heads 65
Hebdige, Dick 109
heavy metal 66, 80; *80-82*
Hell, Richard 90, 91
Hells Angels 67, 68
Hepburn, Audrey *44*
Hill, Teddy 29
Hip cats 28-9; *29*

hip-hop 106
Hippies 29, 49, 63, 64-6, 68, 73, 74, 75, 91, 112; *64-6*
Hippy style 80, 115; *80*
Hipsters 28-9, 30, 31, 41; *29*
Hogg, Pam, 11; *104, 131*
Hollister, California 67
house music 115, 116

Ibiza 115
i-D (magazine) 12, 96
Iggy Pop 90, 91
Indie Kids 122; *122-3*
Italian style 44-5; *44-5*

Jamaica, 58, 76, 78, 109, 110; *109*
James Taylor Quartet 53
Jameson, Frederic 7
Jan & Dean 48
Japan 102, 125
    Acid Jazz fan *121*
    Kajis *16*
    Punk *91*
    Skinhead *71*
jazz 18, 21, 38, 39, 42, 44, 64
John, Elton 25
Jordan *89*
Jubilee (film) 125

Kahn, Jane and Patty Bell *93, 95*
Kajis (Japanese group) *16*
Kensington Market, London *52, 81*
Kerouac, Jack 30; *30*
    On the Road 30
Kesey, Ken 62, 67, 68
Kid Creole *19*
Kidd, Johnny 57
King's Road, London 15, 37, 62, 63, 90; *10, 15, 42, 90, 95*
Kingston, Jamaica 110; *109-11*
Kramer, Stanley 26, 27
Kronfield, Phil 39

Lagerfeld, Karl *49*
La Honda, California 67
Latex (clothes) *103, 104, 128*
Lauren, Ralph *32*
leather (clothing) 80, 83, 103, 104; *81*
Leather Boys 55
Leather Boys, The (film) 47; *47*
leather jackets 10, 11, 68, 83, 89, 91, 92; *90*
Lewis, Jerry Lee 34, 41, 43
Lewis, John 38
Lewis Leathers 10, 47
Liverpool, UK, 101, 116
Liverpool 'Scallies' 101, 116
Louise's nightclub, Soho 91-2, 95; *92*
LSD 62, 64
Lycra 87, 110

McLaren, Malcolm 15, 90, 91, 103; *89*
McGhee, Howard *29*
MacInnes, Colin 50, 51
Mackintosh, Ken 34
Malcolm X 17, 19, 29, 39
Manchester, UK 84, 101, 116
Many Loves of Dobie Gillis, The (TV) 32
Marley, Bob 78; *77*
Martha and the Vandellas 52
Mastroianni, Marcello *45*
Memphis, Tennessee 41

Merry Pranksters, The 62, 63, 67, 68
Meteors, The 102; *102*
Miami, Florida 21, 110
Militant style 108; *108*
Minton's Playhouse, Harlem 28; *28*
Mods 50-3, 54, 55, 60, 61, 63, 69, 70, 74; *51-3*
Modern Jazz Quartet, The 38; *39*
Modernists 38-9; *38, 39*
Monk, Thelonius 28, 29; *28*
'Monsters of Rock' festival 83; *82, 83*
Montana, Claude 11
Moreno, Roddy 71
Mugler, Thierry 11
Mulligan, Gerry 38

New Age Travellers 66, 112-14, 116, 128; *113, 114, 128*
New Edwardians *see* Teddy boys
New Musical Express (magazine) 89
New Orleans 21
New Psychedelics 63
New Romantics 60, 75, 92, 94-6, 97; *94-6*
New York 28, 38, 106, 107, 108; *28 see also* Harlem
New York Dolls 90
New Yorker (magazine) 18
Newburgh Street, London 62, 63
Northern Soul 84-5
Notting Hill Carnival *110*

O'Boogie, Jack *75*
O'Brien, Richard 91
O'Dowd, George *see* Boy George
Oi!(s) 71, 95
On the Road (Kerouac) 30
Otaku (Japanese tribe) 125
Ozbek, Rifat 79

Pablo, Augustus *76*
Pachucos 18, 19
Paris 20, 31
Parker, Charlie 28, 29, 38
Parton, Dolly 25
pavoneggiarsi (male peacock) 45, 51; *45*
Peck, Gregory 44
Perfecto jacket 10, 11, 12, 27, 46-7; *10-12, 26*
Perkins, Carl 41
'Perries' 101, 116
Pervs 103-105; *103-5*
Peterson, Gilles 118, 119; *120*
Philadelphia, Pennsylvania 65
Picasso, Pablo 31
Pimp Look 72, 73
Pop style 63
postmodern theory (of style) 131
Prado, Perez Pantalon *21*
Presley, Elvis 25, 34, 41, 43
Prince Buster 58
Psychedelia 80
Psychedelic Revolution 63
Psychedelics 62-3, 64, 65, 66, 74; *62, 63*
Psychobillies 102; *102*
Public Enemy 108; *108*
Punks 12, 15-16, 37, 43, 70, 71, 75, 87, 89-93, 97, 102, 104, 112, 113, 123; *8, 9, 15, 90, 91, 92, 93*
PVC clothes 92, 103, 104, 105

Quadrophenia (film) 53

Ragga (music and style) 109, 110, 111

Raggamuffins 22, 109-11; *109, 110*
rap 106, 108
Rasta style 78-9
Rastafarians 76-9, 109, 110; *76-9*
Rave 115, 124
Ravers 63, 115-17, 128, 132; *115-17*
Rebel without a Cause (film) 41
Redding, Otis 52
Reed, Lou 90, 91
Reeves, Jim *24*
reggae 78
Rhinestone Cowboys 24, 25, 27, 40; *24*
Rhodes, Zandra 12; *8*
rhythm and blues 41, 42
Richmond, John 11; *131*
Riley, Bridget 62
Riot Grrrls 123
rock 'n' roll 34, 36, 37, 43, 57, 80; *27, 54*
Rockabillies 41-3, 102; *41-3*
Rocker style 80
Rockers 12, 53, 54-7, 67; *54-7*
rocksteady 69
Rocky Horror Show, The 91
Rogers, Roy 24; *23*
Rolling Stones 68; *65, 68*
Rome 44, 45
Roman Holiday (film) 44
rubber (clothing) 92, 103, 104; *103*
Rude Boys 22, 58-60, 69, 78, 110; *58-60*
Rumble Fish (film) 7, 10
Run DMC 107; *106*
Rykiel, Sonia 11

Sallon, Philip 95; *89, 94*
Salt 'N' Pepa *107*
Sartre, Jean-Paul 31
Sampson, Kevin 100-101
'Scallies' 101, 116
Seattle, Washington 122, 123
Selassie, Haile 76
SEX (King's Road shop) 90, 92, 103; *89*
Sex Pistols 15, 90
Shaft (film) 73
SHARP (Skinheads Against Racial Prejudice) 71
Shoom (nightclub), London 116, 117
ska 58, 69, 84
skateboarding 86
Skaterpunks 88
Skaters 86-8; *86-8*
Skinheads 60, 61, 68, 69-71, 100; *14, 69, 70, 71*
Skin Two (club) 104; *103*
sleaze metal 83
Small Faces, The *52*
Smiley T-shirts 92, 115, 124
Smith, Patty 90
Smooths 70
soul (music) 84
sportswear (style) 107, 108, 120
    Casuals 101
    Surfers 48-9
    Skaters 86-8
Steppenwolf 80
Stonehenge 112
Storey, Helen *131*
Strange, Steve 95, 96
Stormy Weather (film) 19; *18*
Stuart, Johnny 12, 47
'Style World' 131, 132
Subterraneans, The (film) 31

Sullivan, Chris 95; *18*
Summer of Love, The 64, 66
Superfly (film) 73
'Supermarket of Style' 124, 130-4; *130, 132-4*
Supremes, The 52
Surfers 48-9, 64, 66, 86; *48, 49*
swing (music) 28
Swinging London 61-3, 65, 74, 75; *61*

Tamla Motown 58
tattoos 13, 123; *13, 70, 93 see also* Dunstable Tattoo Festival
Taylor, Vince 57
Technos 63, 105, 124, 125; *126*
T.E.D.S. (The Edwardian Drape Society) 131; *16*
Teddy boys (and girls) 33-7, 43, 47, 50, 51, 71; *33-7*
teenagers 34, 42, 50
Thomas, Rufus 52
Tokyo *91, 133-5*
    clubs 133, 134
Ton-up Boys 46-7, 55, 57; *46, 47*
Ton-up Girls 47
Top of the Pops (TV) 102, 104, 111
trainers (shoes) 86, 107, 108, 120
trickle-down effect 9, 10
Two-tone (style) 60; *60*
Tulloch, Carol 58

unisex style 74, 75, 123

Versace, Gianni 11, 12; *9, 11, 25*
Vietnam War 66
Vincent, Gene 57
Vogue (magazine) 9, 12

Wagoner, Porter 25; *24*
Wailer, Bunny *79*
Warhol, Andy 61
Warriors, The (film) 14
Weller, Paul *53*
Western style 23-5, 48; *23-5*
Westwood, Vivienne 90, 91, 103; *89, 94*
Who, The 63
Wigan Casino 84, 85; *85*
Wigan, Mark, *84, 85*
Wild Angels, The (film) 67
Wild One, The (film) 10, 26, 29, 46, 67; *26*
Williams, Hank 23-4
Williams, Richard 39
Wolfe, Tom 49, 65, 72-3
World's End, King's Road, London 90
World's End (Westwood's fashion shop) 94

York, Peter 9, 54
Young Soul Rebels 94-5

Zazous 20; *20*
Ziggy Stardust 63, 73, 75
Zombies, The *51*
Zoot suit 17-19; *17, 18, 19*
    riots 19
Zooties 17-19, 27, 28; *17-19*